CHICAGO PUBLI
HAROLD WASHINGTON L

R0002353077

D1324410

53077

THE CHICAGO PUBLIC LIBRARY

LITERATURE & PHILOSOPHY DIVISION

FORM 19

ON MONDAY NEXT

A Comedy in Three Acts

by
PHILIP KING

Author of
SEE HOW THEY RUN
WITHOUT THE PRINCE
ETC.

SAMUEL FRENCH

LONDON
NEW YORK TORONTO SYDNEY HOLLYWOOD

COPYRIGHT 1950 PHILIP KING

This play is fully protected under the copyright laws of the British Commonwealth of Nations, the United States of America, and all countries of the Berne and Universal Copyright Conventions.

All rights are strictly reserved.

It is an infringement of the copyright to give any public performance or reading of this play either in its entirety or in the form of excerpts without the prior consent of the copyright owners. No part of of this publication may be transmitted, stored in a retrieval system, or reproduced in any form or by any means, electronic, mechanical, photocopying, manuscript, typescript, recording, or otherwise, without the prior permission of the copyright owners.

SAMUEL FRENCH LTD, 26 SOUTHAMPTON STREET, STRAND, LONDON WC2E 7JE, or their authorized agents, issue licences to amateurs to give performances of this play on payment of a fee. **The fee must be paid, and the licence obtained, before a performance is given.**

Licences are issued subject to the understanding that it shall be made clear in all advertising matter that the audience will witness an amateur performance; and that the names of the authors of plays shall be included in all announcements and on all programmes.

The royalty fee indicated below is subject to contract and subject to variation at the sole discretion of Samuel French Ltd.

Basic fee for each and every
performance by amateurs   Code H
in the British Isles

In theatres or halls seating 600 or more the fee will be subject to negotiation.

In territories overseas the fee quoted above may not apply. Application must be made to our local authorized agents, or if there is no such agent, to Samuel French Ltd, London.

ISBN 0 573 01318 7

PR
6021
.T275
06

MADE AND PRINTED IN GREAT BRITAIN BY
LATIMER TREND & COMPANY LTD PLYMOUTH
MADE IN ENGLAND

For
HENRY KENDALL
in gratitude and
appreciation

ON MONDAY NEXT

Produced at the Embassy Theatre, London, on April 5th, 1949, and subsequently transferred to the Comedy Theatre, London, on June 1st, 1949, with the following cast of characters—

(in the order of their appearance)

THE PRODUCER (HARRY BLACKER)	*Henry Kendall*
GEORGE	*Charles Lamb*
MAUD BARRON	*Olga Lindo*
JERRY WINTERTON	*Leslie Phillips*
THE AUTHOR	*Richard Goolden*
DAPHNE WRAY	*Beryl Mason*
AVIS CLARE	*Mary Kimber*
JACKSON HARLEY	*Cyril Chamberlain*
MARY MANNERS	*Patricia Page*
SANDRA LAYTON	*Mary Mackenzie*
NORWOOD BEVERLEY	*Liam Gaffney*
A DOCTOR (non-speaking)	
1ST AMBULANCE MAN (two lines)	
2ND AMBULANCE MAN (non-speaking)	

The Play Produced by HENRY KENDALL *and* SHAUN SUTTON

SYNOPSIS OF SCENES

The action takes place on the stage of the Theatre Royal, Drossmouth.

ACT I. Wednesday morning. About ten-fifteen.

ACT II. Ten minutes later.

ACT III. Twenty minutes later.

ACT I

Scene.—*The stage of the Theatre Royal, Drossmouth. Morning.*

As is customary in most repertory theatres, the set of the current play has been partially struck to allow more space for rehearsal. The back wall of the set, representing part of an attractive room in an old country house, has been left standing. It comprises a large recessed french window up L.C., set slightly on an angle, with a straight piece of wall R. of it. In this wall is an arched recess with shelves containing ornaments and a vase of flowers. Piled against this wall and the sides of the french window is the furniture of the current play, covered over with dust sheets. Half-way down R., a large ornate fireplace has been partially struck, but remains in sight. Entrances can be made above and below the fireplace. A single flat has been left unstruck down R. Off up R. can be seen part of the backstage of the theatre, fire hydrants, etc., but a large colourful backing masks the greater part of this side of the backstage. Odd pieces of furniture and a stage lamp stand against the backing. Entrances can be made above and below this backing. A vista backcloth hangs behind the french window. Half-way down L. there is an isolated door braced up by itself. Entrances can be made above, below, or through the door. A single flat has been left unstruck down L. Off, up L., are more backings and packs of scenery, masking the view to the back wall of the stage itself. A rough "prop" table is set at an angle R.C., with chairs R., L., and above it. There is a wooden form up C., just below the pile of covered furniture. Two chairs stand side by side up L.C. An ornate chair from the current play stands L. in the french window recess, and another up L. Off, up L., but in view, is an old sofa with its back to the audience. L. of the sofa are some electrician's stepladders and another stage lamp. There is a bridge R.C. over the orchestra pit, with steps leading down into the auditorium.

(*See the Ground Plan at the end of the Play.*)

From the time the audience enter the theatre, the Curtain *is raised about four feet from the stage, which is lit only by a dim working light. After the house-lights are out there is a pause; then voices are heard off* R. *and the legs of the* Producer *and* George, *the carpenter, come into view below the* Curtain.

Producer (*as he enters*). Well, it's got to be put right by tonight. I told Mary yesterday that that lampshade was dreadful, and she promised it would be changed. And was it? *Was it hell.* George, put the house-lights on, will you?

(George *exits down* L.)

Completely ruins the show. No, that's an exaggeration, the cast
do that.

(*The house-lights and stage lights come on.*)

But that so-and-so lampshade puts the tin hat . . . (*He ducks under
the* CURTAIN *and steps on to the bridge.*)

(*The* PRODUCER *is a man of about forty-five, in a permanent state of
physical tiredness, but mentally he can be a tornado. He is wearing
coloured flannel trousers, a brick-red shirt and a gay tie, and carries a
mass of scripts and odd bits of papers. He has a very definite sense of
humour.*)

(*He sees the audience and stops, aghast.*) Oh, my Lord! I say, I do
beg your pardon, but—I had no idea. (*He surveys the house.*) How
on earth did you all get in? You shouldn't be here, you know. You
shouldn't, really. I mean, we're not giving a performance this
morning. This is a rehearsal—a rehearsal of next week's play. And
as we *never* allow anyone to watch a rehearsal—(*he makes a shoo-ing
gesture with both hands*)—do you mind? (*He pauses expectantly.*) Oh
dear, this is very awkward. I mean—I can't very well throw
you out, can I? It would take too long. What can I do? Better
leave you where you are, I suppose. But you're not going to enjoy
it. Not one little bit. There'll be no proper scenery up; and the
actors and actresses won't be made up or anything like that. (*He
takes a hasty glance under the* CURTAIN.) Have you ever seen an
actress at half past ten in the morning? (*He gives a shocked grimace.*)
Then again, this is only the *second* rehearsal of a brand new play
we're putting on next week. I'm producing it. That's my job with
the Drossmouth Repertory Company—I'm the producer. You've
probably noticed the words "Play produced by Harry Blacker"
on the bills. (*Sadly.*) But as they're usually in such very small type,
I don't suppose you have. Well, anyway, that's me, I'm the
producer, and it's my business to get a fresh play on every week
in this theatre. And what a business. If I were to tell you some of
the things I go through at these rehearsals—but then, if you insist
on staying, there's no need for me to tell you. You'll see for yourselves. (*He pauses and looks around the auditorium.*) I say, are you
quite sure you wouldn't rather go home? (*He pauses.*) All right, on
your own heads be it, but don't say you haven't been warned. Of
course, I just can't understand how you all got in here in the first
place. Or why you should choose this particular morning. (*He
pauses.*) Is it raining outside? Well, as I said before, this is only the
second rehearsal of a brand new play we're presenting for the
first—and I imagine the last—time on any stage on Monday next.
It's a dreadful play. A real shocker. (*He roars with laughter.*) Of
course, I haven't told my cast that. I'm quite certain they think
it's some sort of masterpiece; but then, actors never were any
judge of plays. (*Desperately.*) Look here, *do* please all go away. It's

going to be most frightfully embarrassing for me if you stay. I'm apt to lose my temper on occasions, and I have a feeling that this is going to be an occasion. (*He pauses, then shrugs his shoulders.*) Oh, all right, have it your own way. (*He glances at his wrist-watch.*) What's the time? A quarter past ten. Rehearsals don't begin till half past, so you'll have to amuse yourselves for the next quarter of an hour. I can't stand here chattering to you. I've got a lot of things to do. I've got to go round to the box office and try and touch them for next week's sal . . . (*He breaks off.*) Why should I tell *you* my business. (*He suddenly puts his head under the* CURTAIN *and shouts.*) George. (*He brings his head back and addresses the audience again.*) George is the stage carpenter. (*He puts his head under the curtain and shouts again.*) George.

GEORGE (*off; calling*). Aye, aye, sir.

PRODUCER (*bringing his head back; to the audience*). He was in the Navy once. (*He bobs under the* CURTAIN *and calls.*) George, get the house-lights out and the curtain up.

(GEORGE *enters down* L. *and his legs appear below the* CURTAIN.)

GEORGE. What's the idea?

PRODUCER. What do you mean, "what's the idea?"

GEORGE. We ain't never 'ad the curtain up on a Wednesday morning before.

PRODUCER. Well, it'll be nice to create a precedent, won't it?

GEORGE (*not understanding*). Eh?

PRODUCER. You heard. Oh, for God's sake get the house-lights out and the curtain up. (*He reappears in front of the* CURTAIN.

(GEORGE *pops his head under the* CURTAIN *at the* L. *end.*)

GEORGE. Too arty-arty. That's your trouble.

(*He withdraws his head and exits down* L. *The* PRODUCER *moves on to the bridge.*)

PRODUCER. That was George. He's a grand fellow; we get on very well together—sometimes. Now just one word. For Heaven's sake all of you keep very quiet. Don't let the cast know you're out front or they'll probably refuse to rehearse. After all, it is rather like watching the animals feed, isn't it? Now, I'm going to leave you for ten minutes. And don't forget what I've said. If you *must stay*, then please be quiet. (*He descends the steps into the auditorium, and nearly slips as he does so.*) I shall break my damn neck on this thing one day.

(*He moves to the stalls door and exits. As he does so the* CURTAIN *is drawn fully up and the house-lights go out. There is a pause, then* GEORGE *enters down* L. *He is roughly dressed, with a cloth cap, and dirty white apron. The apron has a large pocket from which protrude a rule, setting plans and other carpenter's odds and ends. He is a grizzled*

old war horse of about sixty, with a walrus moustache. He moves down
C., and begins measuring the stage up towards back C., singing "Roses
of Picardy" quietly to himself. When he is almost up C., MAUD
BARRON enters up R., carrying a shopping basket full of groceries. She is
a woman of fifty, obviously born in a theatrical basket—a good old
trouper. She moves to the table, puts her basket down and checks her
purchases.)

MAUD (*as she enters*). 'Morning, George.

GEORGE. 'Morning, Miss Barron. First—as usual, eh?

MAUD. Yes, George, first as usual. Been round the shops.

GEORGE (*still measuring*). Nice performance yours this week,
Miss Barron.

MAUD. Thank you, George. Bacon—cauliflower . . .

GEORGE (*profoundly*). Ah! I like you in them duchess parts.

MAUD. Do you, George? Liver—sausages . . .

GEORGE (*straightening up and facing MAUD*). My wife always says,
"Put Miss Barron in one of them aristocracy parts and she'll do it
as to the manner born."

MAUD. And haddock. That's very nice of her.

GEORGE (*looking up into the flies*). Which is more than you can
say for a lot of 'em in this 'ere Company.

MAUD. Oh, I don't know. . . .

GEORGE. Maybe you don't, miss. But I do. (*He moves L. of the
table.*) I'll tell you what's wrong with this 'ere Company—too
"arty-arty", that's what it is. All these "amachures" they're getting in these days.

MAUD. They've got to start sometime, George.

GEORGE. But they don't 'ave to start in this theatre, do they?
It's all wrong. And the parts they get. Leading parts before they've
been on the stage five minutes. Weren't like that in the old days.
(*Impressively.*) When I was with Martin 'Arvey, youngsters like
the crowd we've got wouldn't be allowed to play anything but
"Milord, the carriage waits" parts for the first two years.

MAUD. Ah, but times have changed, George.

GEORGE (*moving R. and beginning to measure up R.*). They 'ave an'
all—for the wuss. Oh, there's a letter for you in the rack, miss.

MAUD. For me? (*She turns and moves up R., leaving the groceries on
the table.*) I wonder. . . .

GEORGE (*chuckling*). Perhaps it's a London manager offering
you a big contract.

MAUD. More like someone asking for a big loan.

(JERRY WINTERTON *enters up R. He is a good-looking young man of*
twenty-five, very bright and self-confident. He is carrying a play script
and wears well-creased flannels, sports jacket, a gay shirt and a bright
tartan scarf.)

'Morning, Jerry.

JERRY (*moving below the form up* C.). 'Morning, Maudie.

(MAUD *exits up* R. JERRY *takes off his scarf and drops it with the script on to the form.*)

GEORGE (*measuring up* R.). Martin 'Arvey. Ah, them was the days.

JERRY (*very brightly*). Good morning, Georgie.

GEORGE (*without enthusiasm*). Ah!

JERRY (*still brightly*). What's the matter, George. The old leg playing you up again?

GEORGE (*his back to* JERRY). You leave my leg alone.

JERRY. I wouldn't touch it with a red hot poultice. (*He swings his leg as if to kick* GEORGE.)

(GEORGE *turns suddenly and* JERRY *pretends he was beginning to tap dance. He taps down* R. *to the footlights and across to* L. GEORGE *moves to* R. *of* JERRY.)

GEORGE. Now then. Now then.

JERRY (*still dancing*). What's bitten you?

GEORGE. I've told you abaht that before, Mr Jerry Winterton. Kicking up a dust just arter I cleaned the footlights out.

JERRY. If you cleaned 'em properly, George, there wouldn't be any dust to kick. (*He dances to* R., *passing below* GEORGE. *As he passes him he chucks him under the chin.*) Martin 'Arvey to you.

GEORGE. All right. All right. I'll get me own back. You see if I don't. (*With his back to* JERRY *he bends down to make a mark on the stage.*)

JERRY. George, I warn you. If you start any of your damned hammering when I'm on the stage this morning, I'll take a running kick at you.

(GEORGE *straightens up and turns with an exclamation.*)

How the devil do you expect anyone to remember their lines when you're hammering away at the back of the stage?

GEORGE (*crossing to* JERRY; *angrily*). And 'ow d'you expect me to get next week's scenery ready. 'Ow else am I to get the nails in if I don't use an 'ammer?

JERRY. You might try sitting on them.

GEORGE. Too ruddy particular, some folk. When I was with——

JERRY }
GEORGE } (*together*). Martin 'Arvey.

(GEORGE *turns away in disgust.* JERRY *chuckles and takes out his cigarette case.*)

JERRY. Want a cigarette?

GEORGE (*turning back with alacrity*). Ta.

JERRY. You would.

(*As* GEORGE *takes a cigarette, the* AUTHOR *enters nervously down* L.

He is a mild little man of indefinite age, wearing pince-nez, a black suit, dark tie, dark overcoat and black Homburg hat. He carries a neat, rolled umbrella and a brief-case. He is very shy and stands looking at JERRY *and* GEORGE *apprehensively.)*

JERRY (*nudging* GEORGE). Who's your boy friend?

GEORGE (*looking at the* AUTHOR *in surprise*). Eh? I dunno.

JERRY (*whispering*). I think it's the local undertaker, come for your measurements. Lend him your ruler.

GEORGE. I'll see to him. (*He crosses to the* AUTHOR.) Nah, sir, what can I do for you? (*He pushes the* AUTHOR *gently backwards to* L.)

AUTHOR. Er . . .

GEORGE. Well, we don't allow anyone on the stage, sir.

(GEORGE *and the* AUTHOR *exit down* L. JERRY, *left alone, begins dancing and singing again.* MAUD *enters up* R. *She carries a letter.*)

MAUD. How's Mr Cochran's young gentleman this morning?

JERRY. Younger than ever, ducks. (*He takes a high kick, then immediately clutches his thigh.*) Ouch!

MAUD. Serves you right.

JERRY. Pardon me.

(GEORGE *enters down* L. *and crosses to* JERRY *and* MAUD.)

GEORGE (*catching their attention*). Psst!

JERRY. Well, who is it?

GEORGE (*rather indignantly*). 'E says 'e's an author.

MAUD. Who is?

GEORGE. Chap on the side of the stage. Says 'e wrote the play you're doing next week.

JERRY. Then you can tell him he's no author.

MAUD (*nudging* JERRY). Shut up, you fool. He'll hear you.

GEORGE. What shall I do with him?

JERRY. I'd tell you if Miss Barron wasn't here.

MAUD. I expect he wants to watch the rehearsal.

JERRY. Then God help him. He'd better wait till Harry gets here. (*With glee.*) Oh, yes. Our dear darling producer's going to love this. He just adores having authors making bright suggestions at rehearsals.

(MAUD *laughs, moves to the chair* R. *of the table, sits and re-packs the groceries.*)

Tell him to wait till Mr Blacker comes.

GEORGE. He 'as come. 'E's just gone through to the front of the 'ouse.

JERRY (*loudly*). Then tell him to wait till he comes back.

GEORGE. Orl right. Orl right. I'm not deaf. (*He turns and shouts off* L.) Wait there till Mr Blacker comes back.

(*He exits up* L. *As he does so the* AUTHOR *enters down* L.)

AUTHOR (*timidly*). Thank you so much.

(*He exits down* L.)

MAUD. Author at rehearsal, eh? Wish I'd looked at my part a bit more now. (*She picks up her script.*)

JERRY (*moving to the form and picking up his script*). A bit more. Blimey! I haven't looked at mine at all yet.

MAUD. Oh, Jerry. And you *know* we're supposed to know our first acts on Wednesday morning.

JERRY (*turning the chair* L. *of the table and straddling it*). I know, I know. But I was out at a party last night until two. I meant to learn my first act this morning. Left a note for my landlady, asking her to call me at eight.

MAUD. And did she?

JERRY. Did she hell? The old thing walked in at twenty-five past nine and started playing up because I'd left the front door open and half a dozen cats walked in.

MAUD (*laughing*). Was Norwood at the party?

JERRY. Was he *not*? My dear, he was stinking. He was what my landlady describes as "plastic".

MAUD (*after a slight pause*). Was Sandra there?

JERRY. Good Lord, no. Otherwise Norwood would never have been allowed to get so pickled. Can't think how he got home. On his hands and knees, I suppose.

MAUD. Poor Sandra. She has her hands full with that one.

JERRY (*gaily*). Well, ducks, she took him for better or worse, didn't she?

MAUD. The man's a fool to himself. Such a good actor, too, if he'd only pull himself together. There'll be a bust-up there one of these days, you mark my words.

JERRY. How long have they been married now?

MAUD. Eight or nine years.

JERRY (*without malice*). As long as that? That's a pretty good innings as stage marriages go.

MAUD (*annoyed*). Oh, is it? Well, let me tell you that John and I . . .

(*The* AUTHOR *enters down* L. *He stands just in front of the door waiting to be noticed.*)

JERRY (*rising and laughing*). Oh, you and your John—you're always . . . (*He sees from* MAUD's *face that someone is behind him, and glances over his shoulder. To* MAUD.) There's a peculiar smell of authors about. (*He turns to the* AUTHOR *and speaks curtly as if dismissing him.*) Good morning.

AUTHOR (*uncertainly*). Good morning. I . . .

(*As* JERRY *continues to stare coldly at him the* AUTHOR *backs nervously through the door slam and exits* L.)

MAUD. Jerry, you shouldn't treat the poor man like that. How would you like it if *you* were an author?

JERRY. If I were that particular author I should expect it.

DAPHNE (*off; calling her dog*). Dumpy. Dumpy. Come along. Come along, there's a pet.

JERRY (*breaking up* R.). Oh God! Here's Daphne; and she's brought that lousy poodle of hers to rehearsal again.

AVIS (*off; calling*). Go on, Dumpy. In you go. In you go.

(DAPHNE WRAY *enters down* L. *dragging a small dog on a lead. She also drags on the* AUTHOR *whose sock suspender has become entangled in the lead.* DAPHNE *is a vivacious blonde, in her early twenties, and is wearing a bright dress and a rather silly hat. She has a sling-bag over her shoulder.*)

DAPHNE (*as she enters*). Naughty Dumpy, leaving mother. Come here at once. (*She sees the* AUTHOR *caught up in the lead.*)

(AVIS CLARE *enters up* L. *She is a quiet brunette in her early twenties. She moves to* JERRY, *whispers a few words to him, then crosses and sits on the chair above the table.*)

Now, now, leave that poor little man alone.

(*The* AUTHOR *disentangles his suspender and exits down* L.)

(*She moves down* C. *and calls vaguely into the auditorium.*) Sorry I'm late, darling. (*She turns and moves* L. *of the table. To* MAUD.) 'Lo, darling.

JERRY (*moving* L. *of* DAPHNE). You're *not* late.

DAPHNE (*almost disappointed*). Oh, aren't I?

JERRY. No, dar-*ling*. So you'd better go out and wait five minutes and then make your entrance all over again.

DAPHNE (*picking up her dog*). Jerry Winterton, you're a sarcastic So-and-so.

JERRY. And before Harry gets here—(*he points to the dog*)—you'd better get rid of that damned flue brush.

(GEORGE *enters down* L.)

DAPHNE (*crossing to* GEORGE). George, darling, are you going upstairs?

GEORGE (*gruffly*). No.

DAPHNE. Well, on your way, would you mind shutting Dumpy in our dressing-room. (*Before he has time to protest she puts the dog in his arms.*) Thank you, darling. (*She kisses the dog.*)

(GEORGE *crosses up* R.)

Sweetie Pie, go with Uncle George. And if you ask Uncle George nicely he might give you a little dinky-winky.

GEORGE. Gor, blimey!

(*He exits up* R.)

JERRY (*moving up* C.). Please may I be sick? (*He takes a letter from his pocket and begins to read it.*)

DAPHNE. Oh. Letters. Did anybody notice if there were any for me?

JERRY. Yes, ducky, hundreds.

DAPHNE. Yes, and I'll bet you examined the postmark of every one of them. Of course, if this were a decent theatre, we'd have a stage doorkeeper's office where letters were kept away from the eyes of *all—and—sundry.*

(*She moves and exits up* R.)

JERRY. Who the hell's sundry? Avis, how do you live with that? (*He replaces the letter in his pocket.*)

(*The* AUTHOR *enters down* L.)

It's still with us.

AVIS. Who *is* that?

MAUD (*whispering*). The author, dear. The author of next week's play.

AVIS (*rising; terrified*). You mean the author of—of *this* play? The one we're rehearsing this morning?

JERRY. Of course.

AVIS. But how ghastly. I know I shall dry up all over the place with him watching.

(JERRY *roars with laughter. The* AUTHOR *acutely conscious that he is being discussed, looks round timidly and exits hurriedly down* L. JERRY *crosses to the chair up* L.)

MAUD. Darling, you're only supposed to know your first act anyway. And you *expect* to be prompted quite a lot the first time through.

AVIS. Yes, but . . . (*She takes her script from her handbag and thumbs it through feverishly.*) Don't talk to me for five minutes, anybody, for goodness' sake. (*She moves and sits on the form up* C.)

JERRY (*sitting on the chair up* L.). Heaven preserve me from these conscientious amateurs.

(DAPHNE, *carrying three letters, enters up* R.)

DAPHNE (*to* JERRY). You swine. You said there were lots of letters for me.

JERRY. Weren't there?

DAPHNE. Two. Both of them beginning, "Dear Madam, unless . . ."

JERRY. Oh, I see. Fan mail.

DAPHNE (*moving* R. *of* AVIS). There's one for you, Avis. (*She examines the envelope closely.*) I think it's from your father. The postmark's from your village. (*She hands the letter to* AVIS, *places her bag on the table, then sits in the chair above the table, rather dejectedly examining her own mail.*)

JERRY (*rising*). Hey! Aren't we supposed to be rehearsing this morning? Where's the producer? Where's the stage manager? Where's the rest of the cast?

MAUD. It's only just half past.

JERRY (*flinging his arms out—dramatically*). But I want to act. I want to act.

(*As he says this the* AUTHOR *suddenly enters through the door* L.)

(*He sees the* AUTHOR.) No, I don't!

(JACKSON HARLEY, *the Stage Manager, enters briskly up* R., *followed by his assistant,* MARY MANNERS. JACKSON *is about thirty, well set up and extremely efficient. He is wearing coloured flannels, an open-necked shirt and has a silk scarf tied in a knot around his neck. He carries a script and a piece of board with various papers attached to it by a clip.* MARY *is a student of sixteen; a very plain little wisp of a thing in horn-rimmed spectacles and wearing slacks and shirt and a scarf tied around her head. When she speaks, which is seldom, her voice is a little piping whisper. She carries a tattered stage setting plan.*)

JACKSON (*as he enters; very heartily, in a voice which starts on a high note and gradually comes down the scale*). Good morning, good morning, good morning, good morning. (*He moves down* C.)

(MARY *follows to* R. *of* JACKSON.)

JERRY (*groaning*). Good God!

MARY (*in a little piping voice*). Good morning.

JACKSON. All bright and early this morning, aren't we?

JERRY. We're *early*, anyway.

JACKSON (*clapping his hands authoritatively*). Come along, Mary. Jump to it. Get the stage set.

MARY. Yes, Mr Harley. (*She studies her plan breathlessly, then moves the chair from* L. *of the table to* L.C.)

(JERRY *moves* L. *of* JACKSON.)

JERRY (*with his tongue in his cheek*). Mr—er—Stage Manager. I think there's disaster waiting for you—(*he points off* L.)—over there.

JACKSON. What d'you mean, old boy?

JERRY. Go and see for yourself.

JACKSON (*crossing to* L.). What is it? What is it? Do you want to see me or something?

(*He hustles the* AUTHOR *off and exits down* L.)

MARY (*reading from her plan*). Large refectory table L.C. (*Without looking up she darts to the table, seizes the* L. *end of it and pulls it up* R.C.)

(MAUD *grabs her basket and* DAPHNE *her bag from the table, exclaiming in protest.*)

(*She bumps into* JERRY.) Sorry.

JERRY. You look it.

(MARY *moves the chair* L.C. *to* R. *of the table.* JERRY, *muttering darkly, moves the two chairs from up* L., *one to* L. *of the table and the other above it.* MAUD *places her basket on the floor and studies her script.* AVIS *opens her letter, reads it and starts weeping to herself.*)

MARY (*reading her plan; muttering*). Easy chair by fireplace. (*She moves to* MAUD.) 'Scuse me.

MAUD (*looking up*). What?

MARY. I'm setting the stage and I want that chair.

MAUD (*rising*). Of course, you *would* want this one. (*She picks up her basket and crosses to* JERRY.)

MARY. Clear stage, please. (*She moves the chair a little further* R.)

(DAPHNE *rises, moves her chair up* R., *sits on it again, opens her bag and counts what money she can find in it.* MARY *exits up* R.)

MAUD. Jerry, my sweet, do you *know* you gave me a wrong cue in our big scene last night?

JERRY. Darling, you are getting fussy in your old age. You should thank God I gave you a cue at all.

(MAUD *and* JERRY *exit up* L. *and sit on the sofa off up* L. *with their backs to the audience.*)

DAPHNE (*to herself*). Two and six, three and six, three and six-pence halfpenny . . . oh, God! (*Brightly. To* AVIS.) Darling, I suppose you couldn't lend me two pounds ten?

(AVIS *nods and rises, fighting back her tears.*)

(*She sees the tears and rises.*) Hey, hey! What's the matter, old girl?

(AVIS *collapses sobbing in the chair* R. *of the table.*)

(*She puts her bag on the table, then moves* R. *of* AVIS *and puts her arm around* AVIS's *shoulder.*) Come on, come on. Tell the old girl what's wrong. Unless, of course, it's something . . .

AVIS (*through her sobs*). Daphne—I've got to give in my notice—and go home.

DAPHNE (*surprised*). What? Oh, what a shame. Why?

AVIS. It's father. He can't do without me. He *has* tried, poor dear, but ever since mother died, and I went to London to the dramatic school, he's just had a succession of housekeepers and daily women. I've felt awful sometimes when I've thought of him in that vicarage—all on his own—but I *did* want to go on with this.

DAPHNE (*genuinely sympathetic*). Poor Avis.

AVIS. I know I'm not a great actress—I'll never be a star or anything like that. . . .

DAPHNE. Darling, be your age. You don't have to be a great

B

actress to be a star. You can get there with other qualifications far less exacting. (*She pauses, then looks at* Avis.) Oh dear, now I've shocked you, haven't I?

Avis. No, of course you haven't. That's one of the things I like so much about the theatre. People do say what they think. When I think of going back to that dreary little village full of repressions and small talk . . .

Daphne. But think of waking up in the morning to the smell of green fields and hay and—things—instead of the smell of stale grease paint that you should have taken off the night before and didn't.

Avis. But I love the smell of stale grease paint. Oh, I know I'm only a beginner. This is my first job, and I suppose the glamour hasn't worn off yet.

Daphne (*derisively*). Glamour. Call this glamour? Sweating your inside out in a dump like this? (*She moves below the table.*) Learning a fresh part every week and cramming in lines till you don't know whether you're on your head or your what's-it?

Avis. But why did you go on the stage if you don't like it?

Daphne. Well, the theatre's in my blood really—Mother was a programme seller at the Kilburn Empire. (*She moves to the table and perches herself on the L. end of it.*) So it seemed kind of natural that I should come into the business. (*She picks up her handbag and, while speaking, takes a compact from the bag and powders her nose.*) I started in a super-musical called *Bare Skins and Blushes*, so you see this weekly repertory racket isn't really my line at all. Of course, we've all got to live, so naturally I take what comes along, but—I don't want to blow my own trumpet, duckie—but I do wish you could have seen my Aladdin last Christmas at Stockton-on-Tees.

(Avis *bursts into fresh sobbing.*)

(*She looks at* Avis, *surprised.*) Well, it wasn't as bad as all that. Oh, my dear. Aren't I a selfish little swine, talking about my triumphs when you're so upset. Cheer up, Avis, and don't worry. It may never happen. Something might turn up.

Avis (*rising and breaking* c.). But it *will* happen—and I know exactly what will turn up. A curate. And I shall marry it. And I shall spend the rest of my life organizing church bazaars and garden fêtes and—maybe, Amateur Theatricals. Oh, God!

(*She turns and exits hurriedly up* R., *sobbing.*)

Daphne (*to herself—it is rather a pleasant thought*). I wouldn't mind marrying a curate.

(Jackson *enters down* L. *followed by the* Author.)

Jackson (*moving* c.; *irritably*). Yes, yes, yes. We'll go into all that later. (*He turns and finds the* Author *still with him.*) Yes—well

—perhaps you'd better wait till Mr Blacker arrives. (*He glares at the* AUTHOR.)

(*The* AUTHOR *smiles wretchedly ard retreats through the door* L. *where he remains pottering about.* MARY, *carrying a small prompt table enters hurriedly up* R., *moves down* C., *sets the table down, then turns, rushes up* R. *and exits.*)

(*He places the board with his sheaves of notes attached to it on to the table.*) What the *hell* does he want to turn up for?

DAPHNE. Who is it, Jacko?

JACKSON (*moving to* R. *of her, script in hand*). Just the author of *this* little travesty, come to watch the rehearsals. Feels that as it's the first production he ought to be here to give us a hand. Of course, he doesn't understand the first thing about weekly "Rep". Seemed to imagine that everyone would know their parts backwards by today. (*He laughs.*) He went quite pale when I told him we'd only know our first act.

DAPHNE (*derisively*). Ha, ha.

(*The* AUTHOR *enters up* L.)

JACKSON. What's biting you?

DAPHNE. First act. My dear, I don't know a line. (*She goes off into whoops of laughter but stops abruptly when she suddenly sees the* AUTHOR *a few feet away from her.*)

(*The* PRODUCER *enters through the stalls door. At the same time* MARY *enters up* R. *carrying two chairs.*)

PRODUCER (*approaching the bridge*). Morning, Jacko. Everyone here?

JACKSON (*moving to the prompt table*). Everyone except Sandra and Norwood, and they're not on until nearly the end of the act. Norwood's always late, anyway.

PRODUCER (*coming over the bridge*). Right. Then let's begin, shall we? (*As he crosses the bridge he turns to the audience and says "Shh!". He then moves to the prompt table, looks at it, then at the auditorium.*) I think we'll have the prompt table at the side this morning. (*He moves a little up* C.)

(MARY *puts the two chairs down* R.)

JACKSON (*surprised*). What?

PRODUCER. Yes, I think we will. (*To* MARY.) Mary, dear, move the table to the side of the stage, will you?

MARY (*rushing to the prompt table; brightly*). Yes, Mr Blacker. (*She takes the table down* R.)

JACKSON (*noticing the* AUTHOR *hovering down* L.; *to the* PRODUCER). Oh, by the way, Harry.

PRODUCER. Yes? (*To* MARY.) No, no, dear, not there. The *other* side.

(MARY *moves the table down* L., *returning for the chairs.* JACKSON *and the* PRODUCER *converse inaudibly; it is obvious that they are discussing the* AUTHOR. *It is also obvious to the* AUTHOR *that he is being told about. The* PRODUCER *and* JACKSON *dart surreptitious glances at him, making him more sheepish than ever.*)

PRODUCER. All right, I'll deal with him. (*He suddenly yells.*) Stand by, everybody please. Act One.
MARY. Stand by, please.
JACKSON (*moving up* R.; *calling*). George!

(*He exits* R.)

PRODUCER (*moving to the* AUTHOR). Now, Mr—er—er——
AUTHOR (*agreeing*). Yes.

(MARY *exits down* L.)

PRODUCER. I am Harry Blacker, the Producer.
AUTHOR. I'm so glad to meet you.
PRODUCER. Er—yes. (*With a jocular note in his voice.*) Rather hitting below the belt, you know, turning up for the second rehearsal like this. I'm afraid you'll find your play in a very rough state this morning.

(MAUD *rises, enters by the french windows, and sits on the form up* C.)

AUTHOR (*anxiously*). Well, you see, Mr Blacker, I thought that I might . . .
PRODUCER (*quite unheeding*). Quite, quite. (*He crosses below the* AUTHOR *to* L. *and calls.*) Oh, Mary.

(MARY *enters down* L.)

Don't forget to tell the electrician he's got to get that damned lampshade changed for tonight, will you?
MARY. Shall I tell him now, Mr Blacker?
PRODUCER. Yes, if you can find him.
MARY. Yes, Mr Blacker.

(*She exits down* L.)

(*Off; calling.*) 'Lectrics, 'lectrics.
PRODUCER (*turning*). Now let me see, where were we?
AUTHOR. Oh well, I was just saying . . .

(JACKSON *enters up* R. *and moves* C.)

PRODUCER (*patting the* AUTHOR *affectionately on the back*). Just a minute, old boy, do you mind? Jackson, can't we get started now?
JACKSON (*calling*). Stand by, everyone, *please*. (*He yells.*) Mary. Come and get on the prompt book. Where is she?

(DAPHNE *rises, moves to the form up* C. *and sits* R. *of* MAUD.)

PRODUCER. She's gone to find "electrics". I told her yesterday that I wanted that lampshade changed in Act One. The damned thing absolutely kills the set. Who the devil chose it in the first place?

JACKSON (*turning to the* PRODUCER). As a matter of fact, I did.

PRODUCER. Oh, really, Jacko, I thought you had better taste than that.

(*The* AUTHOR *is becoming sandwiched between* JACKSON *and the* PRODUCER.)

JACKSON (*annoyed*). But, damn it all, you said you liked it when it came from the shop.

PRODUCER (*irritatingly*). Calm, Jacko, keep calm. I may have said I liked it when it came from the shop, but I just don't like it when it's on the stage, that's all.

(*The* AUTHOR *is completely squashed between them.*)

JACKSON (*more annoyed*). But Hell's bells. You passed it at the dress rehearsal.

PRODUCER (*with magnificent patience*). My dear Jacko, I may have *adored* it when it came from the shop, I may have *swooned* over it at the dress rehearsal, but I *loathed* every blasted tassel on it when the curtain went up on it on Monday night, so (*sweetly*) with your permission we will have it changed. (*More sweetly.*) O.K., dear boy?

JACKSON (*roaring*). Yes. (*He stumps to the prompt table and sits in the chair nearest the prompt corner.*) Now, can we get on, please?

(*The* PRODUCER *wanders down* R. *and exits. The* AUTHOR *is left standing in the middle of the stage.*)

(*He tries to assert himself.*) Stand by everyone. Act One. (*He shouts.*) Clear the stage, please!

(*The* AUTHOR *remains standing in the middle of the stage.*)

(*He bellows.*) *Clear the stage, please.* (*Then, as the* AUTHOR *stands blinking pathetically, he addresses him with a tremendous attempt at patience.*) Do you mind, old boy, you're standing on the *set.*

AUTHOR (*very unhappy and trying to see what he was supposed to be standing on*). Oh, I beg your pardon—I was just waiting to have a word with Mr Blacker. (*He moves to the chair above the prompt table and sits in it.*)

JACKSON (*rising quickly*). No, no, old boy. For Heaven's sake, not there.

AUTHOR (*rising quickly as if bitten*). I beg your pardon. Not there?

JACKSON. No, old boy. You can't possibly. (*With awe and reverence, and almost stroking the chair.*) That is—the *producer's* chair. (*He moves it an inch or two further down towards the footlights.*)

AUTHOR (*regarding the chair rather as he would look at the Crown jewels*). Oh. (*Then, in a whisper.*) Yes—of course. (*He looks around for another chair, but there isn't one. So he stands unhappily down* L., *clutching his brief-case, from which he now extracts a script.*)

(NOTE: *At no time does the* PRODUCER *ever sit in his chair. It remains isolated.*)

JACKSON (*busy with his prompt script*). Daphne. You begin this act, don't you?

DAPHNE. Oh, do I? (*She rises hurriedly and sends her handbag flying. Its contents are scattered around her. She gets on her hands and knees and picks them up.*)

JACKSON (*reading from his script*). "An attractive maid enters from the dining-room."

DAPHNE. An *attractive* maid. Darling, that *must* be me. (*She has just finished picking everything up when her handbag slips in her hands and the contents are scattered once more.*)

(*The* PRODUCER *enters down* R.)

PRODUCER. Come along, dear. Stand by.

(*The* AUTHOR *moves* L. *of the door.* DAPHNE *once more recovers the contents of the handbag, but this time manages to get her leg through the sling of it.*)

DAPHNE (*hopping about*). I'm so sorry.
PRODUCER (*yelling*). Leave it. Leave it. For Heaven's sake let's get on.

(DAPHNE *gets her leg free, puts her handbag on the form, picks up her script then stands uncertainly* C., *not sure where she ought to enter.*)

PRODUCER (*irritably*). Well, go on, go on. Make your entrance.
DAPHNE (*a little nervously*). Er—where do I come on from?
AUTHOR (*poking his head through the door*). The dining-room. (*He retreats again through the door.*)

(*Everyone reacts to his sudden appearance and disappearance.*)

DAPHNE. Oh yes, of course, thank you. Silly of me. (*To the* PRODUCER.) Sorry, darling, I'm all blah this morning. I've just had the most extraordinary letter from a boy I used to know in the Air Force. His wife won't let him come up for the week-end. (*She laughs gaily. But her smile fades under the unrelenting stare of the* PRODUCER.) Now—*which* is the bathroom?

(*There is a tense silence during which nobody moves but the* PRODUCER *who, in an attempt to control his temper, leans against the proscenium* R. *and slowly beats one clenched fist against it. At last he turns.*)

PRODUCER (*sombrely*). There is *no* bathroom. (*He moves to* DAPHNE.) Come here, my pet. Come on. Come to Daddy. You *were* at rehearsal yesterday, weren't you?

(DAPHNE *can only nod.*)

(*A little louder.*) And I *did* describe the set to you—to everybody, didn't I?

(DAPHNE *nods again.*)

(*Louder still.*) Then can you tell me why in the name of thunder I've got to go to the trouble of explaining it all over again just for *your* benefit?

(DAPHNE *is silent.*)

(*He yells.*) Do you think I've got nothing better to do than waste my time on half-witted juveniles?

(*There is a scuffle offstage and* JERRY *enters hurriedly up* L.)

JERRY. Somebody calling *me*?

(MAUD *quickly* "*shh's*" JERRY *who moves up and sits* R. *of* MAUD *on the form.*)

PRODUCER (*controlling himself, but still angry*). All right. All right. For the sake of Miss Daphne Wray, I will describe the scene again. Give me your hand, dear. (*He crosses* DAPHNE, *takes her left hand in his right, and leads her* L.) The scene is the hall in Sir Some-body Somebody-or-other's country house. . . .
    AUTHOR (*from behind the door*). Sir John Frazer-Forbes.
    PRODUCER (*to* JACKSON). Thank you, Jacko. (*He swings open the door and leads* DAPHNE *through.*) Down left——

(*The* AUTHOR *is knocked backwards by the opening door.*)

—is the door to the study. Got that?

(DAPHNE *nods.*)

(*He leads her below the door to* C. *and points up stage.*) Up centre, here, is an eight-foot opening with a large latticed window at the back. Got that?

(DAPHNE *nods. The* AUTHOR, *feverishly exploring his script, follows them around.*)

(*He leads her* R.) Half-way down right is the fireplace. And down right is the entrance to the bathroom—(*he corrects himself*)—the dining-room, damn you. Got that?

(DAPHNE *nods.*)

(*He leads her* C.) And that's the lot. Now can we get started?

(*He keeps hold of* DAPHNE'S *hand throughout the next episode.*)

AUTHOR (*in a very audible whisper*). Mr Blacker. The staircase.
PRODUCER (*unheeding*). Now is everybody standing by?
AUTHOR. Mr Blacker, you've forgotten the staircase.
PRODUCER (*not knowing who it is, glaring around*). What's that?

Who is it that keeps chattering? Jacko, you're the stage manager, can't you keep them quiet?

AUTHOR (*nervous but desperate*). I'm sorry, Mr Blacker, I'm afraid it was me. (*He runs behind the* PRODUCER *and pops up on his* L.) I just wanted to call your attention to the fact that you've forgotten to mention the staircase.

PRODUCER (*blankly*). What? What staircase?

AUTHOR. The one in the set. (*He opens his script.*) I described it at the beginning of the play, surely? (*He finds the place.*) Yes, here it is. (*He reads.*) "Dominating the whole scene is a magnificent Adams staircase which sweeps majestically down the entire length of the back and right walls."

PRODUCER (*moving towards the proscenium* R.). Oh yes, but that's cut.

AUTHOR (*blankly*). Cut?

PRODUCER. Yes, definitely cut.

AUTHOR (*babbling*). But, Mr Blacker, it can't be.

PRODUCER (*swinging round ominously, and at the same time swinging* DAPHNE *round with him*). *Why* can't it be, if *I* say so?

AUTHOR. But, Mr Blacker, it's so essential to the end of the play. (*He hastily turns over the pages of his script.*) At the end there's that terribly dramatic moment when Lady Frazer-Forbes, already heartbroken at the death of her dog, appears at the top of the staircase and, leaning over the balustrade, sees her husband locked in the arms of the gardener's wife and, falling in a dead faint, crashes down the staircase to her death. (*He indicates the action most dramatically.*)

(*There is a pause. Then the* PRODUCER *and* DAPHNE *move up* R. *to where* MAUD *is seated on the form.*)

PRODUCER (*in a dead voice*). Maudie.

MAUD (*rising*). Me?

PRODUCER. Yes, dear. Are you good at crashing down magnificant Adams staircases to your death?

MAUD. Well, dear, I'll try anything once. (*She resumes her seat.*)

PRODUCER (*grimly*). Not this time you won't. I'm sorry, my dear sir, but Miss Maud Barron is a character actress, *not* a Japanese acrobat. (*He takes the* AUTHOR *by the arm and leads him down* C., DAPHNE *still in tow.*) Now, please. You must be reasonable. In any case we haven't anything in our stores remotely resembling a magnificent Adams staircase. (*Then suddenly clicking his fingers.*) Wait a minute. Jacko. What happened to those stairs we used in *Rebecca* last week?

JACKSON. I think they're kicking around the back somewhere.

PRODUCER. Well, go and see if you can find them, will you?

(JACKSON *rises and exits down* L. *During the next speeches he can be seen looking for the staircase, gradually working his way round the back and off* R.)

AUTHOR. I do hope you don't think I'm being difficult, Mr Blacker.

PRODUCER (*beaming*). My dear sir. Of course not.

AUTHOR. You see, the staircase is so very important. (*He raises his umbrella towards the back of the stage, narrowly missing the PRODUCER.*) I visualized it running the length of the back wall, and curving up there—(*the umbrella passes over the PRODUCER's head again narrowly missing him*)—and coming down almost to the foot-lights.

PRODUCER (*agreeably*). Most effective. Most effective.

AUTHOR. I'm so glad you agree with me.

(*There is a loud crash as JACKSON man-handles the steps off stage. The PRODUCER jumps and moves down R. as JACKSON drags on a wooden structure of four steps with a small rostrum at their head. The whole thing is in a very battered condition. JACKSON drags it C.*)

PRODUCER (*heartily*). Ah! Here we are. The very thing.

(*The AUTHOR regards the steps with horror.*)

Now let me see, where can we put it? Ah yes. (*He moves slightly up R. with DAPHNE.*) We'll have the stairs running off up right. Put it there, Jacko.

JACKSON (*to the AUTHOR*). Would you mind giving me a hand? Bit on the heavy side.

(*JACKSON and the AUTHOR carry the flight of steps to a position three-quarters of the way up R. Entrances can still be made above and below the steps. The AUTHOR lets his end go and drops it on his toe.*)

PRODUCER. Thanks a lot. (*Very heartily.*) That's right. About there, I think. Splendid. (*To the AUTHOR.*) There's your stair-case. Happy?

AUTHOR (*almost speechless*). I . . .

PRODUCER (*moving C., pulling DAPHNE with him and bearing the protesting AUTHOR before him*). That's fine. Now, come along, everybody, come along. We're losing momentum. Speed and punch. That's what we've got to get into this play. Speed and punch. Now stand by, everybody.

(*The PRODUCER and DAPHNE stop C. JACKSON hurries to his corner down L., hustling the AUTHOR still further L.*)

Who opens the play?

(*The AUTHOR hangs his umbrella on the chair R. of the prompt table.*)

JACKSON. Daphne. (*He sits at the prompt table.*)

PRODUCER (*yelling*). Daphne. Where the devil's Daphne?

(*He swings round and round searching for DAPHNE, who swings round with him.*)

Why can't people stand by.

DAPHNE (*in a small coy voice*). I'm here, darling.

PRODUCER (*starting and looking around*). What? Good Lord! Have I been dragging you round with me all this time? *No!* (*He goes off into peals of laughter.*)

DAPHNE (*also hooting with laughter*). Yes, darling.

PRODUCER (*shrieking with mirth*). Well, I'm damned. Well, of all the . . .

(JACKSON *regards them sourly from his seat at the prompt table. The remainder of the people on the stage merely look glum, particularly the* AUTHOR.)

Oh, dear. Oh, dear. Nothing like starting the morning with a good laugh. (*He catches sight of* JACKSON's *sour expression and stops laughing.*) Oh, my God! (*He moves to his position down* R.) Now, come along, Daphne, make your entrance.

(DAPHNE *runs up* C.)

No, no, darling. From the dining-room. (*He indicates down* R.) Remember?

DAPHNE (*moving down* R.). Oh, yes.

JACKSON. Curtain up.

(DAPHNE *pantomimes opening a door and closing it after her, takes a quick glance at her script, then moves* R.C. *and goes through the actions of dusting ornaments on an imaginary mantelpiece.*)

DAPHNE (*explaining*). Dusting ornaments on mantelpiece.

PRODUCER (*agreeably*). Very good, dear.

JACKSON (*referring to his script*). You're supposed to be humming a song, too.

DAPHNE. Oh, yes, of course. (*She sings, rather shrilly, the first bars of* "One Fine Day".)

PRODUCER (*curtly*). Cut the humming.

JACKSON (*marking his script with a pencil*). Humming out.

(DAPHNE *looks annoyed. She then moves above the table, puts her script down and begins to make strange gestures in the air in front of her.*)

(NOTE: *The acting* "in the play" *should be very, very slightly exaggerated, but at no time should it be burlesqued.*)

PRODUCER (*after watching for a moment*). I didn't know there was an under-water ballet in this play. What exactly are you supposed to be doing, dear?

DAPHNE. Arranging flowers in a bowl.

PRODUCER (*in a depressed voice*). I see. Carry on.

(DAPHNE *continues to arrange flowers for a very considerable time.*)

(*At last—wildly.*) Good God! You don't arrange flowers all night, do you?

DAPHNE (*snappily*). I'm waiting for the butler to come on. (*She picks up her script.*)

PRODUCER (*yelling*). Butler. Where's the butler? (*He moves to C. between the steps and the table.*) For Heaven's sake stand by.

JACKSON. Oh, come on, who's playing the butler? (*He refers to his script.*) I do wish people would stand by. (*He finds the cast list.*) Oh, Lord, it's me. (*He rises hastily and runs to the top of the steps.*)

PRODUCER (*muttering*). Come along, come along, you of all people. You should set an example.

(JACKSON *stands holding the prompt script balanced on one hand like a tray. The* PRODUCER *stares at it.*)

JACKSON (*explaining*). Tray.

PRODUCER (*going back to his corner*). Oh.

JACKSON (*reading from his script*). "Ahem. Ahem." (*He pronounces it as the name of a Biblical character.*)

PRODUCER (*sarcastically*). I didn't know this was a Biblical play.

JACKSON (*getting it and laughing*). Oh, yes, of course. (*He coughs.*) "Ahem. Ahem."

DAPHNE (*turning with a start of surprise and speaking in an extremely "refined" voice*). "Lor, Mr 'Iggins, how you startled me."

(*The* PRODUCER *lets out a cry of strangled misery. Everyone looks at him.*)

What's the matter? Didn't I say it right?

PRODUCER. No, it isn't that. (*He leans against the proscenium R., hands in trousers pockets, shoulders hunched, thinking deeply. Then he begins to walk slowly back and forwards across the front of the stage. He speaks quietly and reminiscently as he goes.*) Years ago, when I was a very little boy, my mother used to take me to the theatre every week. (*He glares at the* AUTHOR.) Awful old dramas we saw. But one thing about them lingers in my memory to this day. In each and every one of them, when the curtain went up on Act One, a maid would enter, and after dusting ornaments on the mantelpiece, she would arrange flowers in a bowl. Then—the butler would enter—cough—and (*his voice rises to a crescendo*) as sure as God made little apples the maid would turn and say "Lor, Mr 'Iggins, 'ow you startled me." (*He pauses, then speaks quietly but almost venomously to* DAPHNE.) Your first line is *out.*

JACKSON (*busy with script and blue pencil; very rapidly*). "Lor, Mr 'Iggins 'ow you startled me"—*out.*

PRODUCER (*turning to the* AUTHOR *with great charm and joviality*). You don't mind, old boy, do you?

(*The* AUTHOR *gulps and shakes his head.*)

JACKSON (*in part*). "Rose. 'Er Ladyship wants to see you."

(JACKSON *is a stage director, not an actor. His rendering of the Butler is stolid and toneless.*)

DAPHNE (*moving below the table*). "Her Ladyship must wait. I've only one pair of—(*she turns a page*)—hands, as well she knows."

(*The* PRODUCER *gives a little whimper.* DAPHNE *turns and looks at him.*)

PRODUCER (*in a voice of one damned and doomed for ever more*). No, no, it's all right. You're doing fine. Fine. (*He buries his head dazedly in his hand, leaning against the door slam.*)

JACKSON (*in part*). "That's no way to speak of your mistress— my girl."

DAPHNE (*as herself*). Do you stand on those stairs all through this scene?

JACKSON. I shall come down when it tells me in the script and not before.

(*The* PRODUCER *looks over the* AUTHOR'S *shoulder at the* AUTHOR'S *script.*)

DAPHNE (*witheringly*). I see. And I play all the time with my back practically to the audience. (*With an exaggerated shrug of the shoulders.*) Oh, don't mind me.

PRODUCER (*coming to; brightly*). Ah! Now that was good. Keep that line just like that.

DAPHNE. What line?

PRODUCER. "Oh, don't mind me." Keep it just as you said it.

DAPHNE (*furiously*). That wasn't a line in the play at all. I was talking to him. (*She points to* JACKSON.)

PRODUCER (*reflectively*). Hmm! Pity. All right. Carry on.

DAPHNE (*muttering angrily*). Really, with all these interruptions I shall go mad.

PRODUCER (*sternly*). Now then. I don't want any of *your* temperaments. Get on with it.

JACKSON (*in part; tonelessly*). "That's no way to speak of your mistress—my girl."

PRODUCER (*crossing to* L. *of the steps*). No, and that's no way to speak that line, either, my boy. (*Very earnestly and grandly.*) Jacko, Jacko, you *must* try and remember that this man you're playing— he's a *butler.* Make him *pompous, pompous.* Very conscious of his exalted position in the household. Make this one the perfect butler, so perfect that if you met him walking down the street stark naked you would point to him and say, "That man is a butler!" (*He points dramatically down* L. *at the* AUTHOR.) See what I mean? After all, this man has probably been butlering in the household of Sir Somebody Something . . . (*He snaps his fingers.*)

AUTHOR (*at the risk of his life*). Sir John Frazer-Forbes.

PRODUCER (*with a glance at the* AUTHOR). You're perfectly right. (*He breaks* R.) In the household of Sir Foozlum-Foozlum for the past twenty years.

AUTHOR (*blurting out*). Oh, but he *hasn't.*

(*The* PRODUCER *stops dead in his tracks, with his back to the* AUTHOR.)

PRODUCER (*very quietly*). Who hasn't what?
AUTHOR (*oblivious to the rising tension*). This butler. He hasn't been with the Frazer-Forbes for the last twenty years.

(*In the tense pause that follows, the* PRODUCER *slowly turns and faces the* AUTHOR.)

PRODUCER (*ominously*). No?
AUTHOR (*blandly*). Oh dear, no. Don't you remember, Mr Blacker. Later in the play it comes out in the dialogue that he isn't a butler at all, but Hampstead Harry, a notorious jewel thief.

(*There is a tense silence, but the storm does not break. The* PRODUCER, *after a brief but tense pause, merely returns to his position down* R.)

PRODUCER (*in a cold, hard voice*). Carry on.
JACKSON (*exactly as before*). "That's no way to speak of your mistress—my girl."

(JACKSON *and everyone else except the* AUTHOR, *looks toward the* PRO-DUCER *expecting they don't quite know what. The* PRODUCER *is conscious of their stares, but looks out front, unable to face them. At last, trying to save his face, he speaks witheringly.*)

PRODUCER. Is that the end of the play?
DAPHNE (*gulping and resuming her part very quickly*). "Mistress. A fine mistress she is, I must say. No better than she ought to be, if you ask me."
JACKSON (*in part*). "But I'm not asking you—my girl."
DAPHNE (*in part*). "I've worked for better families than this in my time, I'll be bound."
JACKSON (*in part*). "That's as may be—my girl, but while you're working for this one, I'll thank you to speak with respect for your betters."
DAPHNE (*in part*). "Betters, indeed. We're all human."

(*There is a pause.*)

JACKSON (*as himself*). Well, I don't say anything.
DAPHNE (*turning over a page; in part*). ". . . beings, I should hope."

(*The* PRODUCER *groans.*)

JACKSON. Now this is where I come down the stairs. (*He comes down.*)
DAPHNE (*darkly*). And about time.
JACKSON (*in part*). "Human beings we may be, Rose, but we all 'ave our stations in life. Now, you—my girl . . ."

(*The* PRODUCER *gives an agonized cry.*)

PRODUCER. Just one moment. (*He crosses slowly to the* AUTHOR, *holding out his hand as he goes.*) Excuse me, would you lend me your script for a moment. (*He takes the* AUTHOR's *script, moves* C. *and makes a pretence of studying a page, then flicks over to the next one. All eyes are on him and he knows it. He slowly and deliberately flicks through the pages, one by one, flicking over each page with a smart gesture.*)

(*The* AUTHOR *watches him apprehensively, but is at last compelled to speak.*)

AUTHOR (*nervously*). Can I help you, Mr Blacker? What is it you're trying to find?

PRODUCER (*very deliberately*). The plot.

(DAPHNE *giggles. She relaxes and sits on the table.*)

MAUD (*rising*). I'm getting out of this.

AUTHOR (*bewildered*). The plot?

(MAUD *exits through the french window.*)

PRODUCER. Yes. Most plays have one, you know. This would appear to be the exception. (*He flicks one more page.*) Ah, no. Wait a minute. I think I've found the beginning of a plot *here*. On page twenty-two. At the moment we are on page—(*he flicks back the pages again*)—*one.* (*He turns to* JACKSON. *Heavily.*) Jacko, have you your blue pencil?

(JACKSON *hands the* PRODUCER *a pencil.*)

AUTHOR (*greatly perturbed*). Mr Blacker, you're not going to cut any of the dialogue, are you?

(*The* PRODUCER *blue pencils several pages of the script.*)

PRODUCER (*after staring at the* AUTHOR; *to the Company*). Relax, everybody.

(DAPHNE *rises from the table and moves above it.* JACKSON *moves above the table and offers* DAPHNE *a cigarette. They smoke together.* JERRY *rises and exits up* R.)

(*To the* AUTHOR, *with great charm.*) Now, my dear sir. What is your name, by the way? (*He looks at the front of the script.*) Oh, no, it *can't* be. (*He roars with laughter, and then remembers himself.*) I'm terribly sorry. (*He hands the script to the* AUTHOR, *then takes him gently by the right arm and walks him slowly about the stage.*) This, I rather imagine, is your first play. Correct?

(*As they pass the chair* R. *of the prompt table the* PRODUCER *picks up the* AUTHOR's *umbrella.*)

AUTHOR (*conscious that he is being dragged about the stage*). Er—yes.

PRODUCER (*leaving the* AUTHOR R.). Yes. Well, you all have to begin sometime, I suppose. Mind you, I think this is a very good play—for a first. But—(*with a gesture*)—it has its faults.

AUTHOR (*apprehensively*). Er—has it?

PRODUCER (*leading the* AUTHOR C.). It has indeed.

AUTHOR. Oh.

(JACKSON *moves down* L. *and sits on his chair.* DAPHNE *sits up* L.)

PRODUCER (*swinging the umbrella as a golf club*). Yes. When the directors of this theatre, who are also the Play Selection Committee, as perhaps you know. . . .

AUTHOR (*innocently*). Oh, yes. My aunt is one of the Directors.

PRODUCER (*heavily*). Your aunt. Quite. (*He pauses.*) Well, as I was saying, when the Directors of this theatre handed me your play and told me I *had* to put it on—(*he swings the inverted umbrella viciously and just misses the* AUTHOR)—I—er—made so bold as to point out that the play had certain faults. One of the Directors, a Mrs Bellinger—(*with great venom*)—your aunt, I believe . . .

AUTHOR. Yes.

PRODUCER. Yes. Mrs Bellinger took the trouble to come and see me personally. We had quite a long and interesting chat together. I told her what *I* thought about the play and she told me what *she* thought about the play and, quaintly enough, we found that we both held entirely different points of view. However, to cut a long story short, Mrs Bellinger did in the end agree that if I found any major faults in the play, I should do my best to rectify them.

AUTHOR (*apprehensively*). That's very kind of you, Mr Blacker. Er—do you think you *have* found a major fault?

PRODUCER (*slowly—as if the answer might be "No"*). Er—yes.

AUTHOR. Oh. Er—what?

PRODUCER. The first twenty pages.

AUTHOR (*staggered*). The first twen . . . But what do you suggest we should do about it, Mr Blacker?

PRODUCER (*airily*). Cut them out.

AUTHOR (*horrified*). Cut them out. But, Mr Blacker, that will ruin the play.

PRODUCER (*thoughtfully, with a wealth of meaning*). No—I don't think it will make any difference to the success of the play.

AUTHOR (*babbling*). But—but—there are only *thirty* pages in the first act. If you cut out the first twenty, that will leave you with only ten.

PRODUCER (*having checked the* AUTHOR's *arithmetic on his fingers*). So it does. (*He takes the* AUTHOR's *right arm and begins walking him round the stage again. They move* R.) Never mind. You will write us another twenty pages and we shall rehearse them tomorrow morning.

AUTHOR (*baffled and bewildered*). But—but, Mr Blacker—I couldn't really—I couldn't—not in the time.

PRODUCER (*leading the* AUTHOR *to* L.; *heartily*). Nonsense, my dear sir. Nonsense. With an alert brain like yours. Why I remember once (*they turn and walk towards the steps*) I was in the original production of an Edgar Wallace play, (*they walk up the steps on to the rostrum*) Edgar came to rehearsal one day and the Producer told him that he was dissatisfied with the first twenty-*nine* pages What did Edgar do? Without a murmur he retired to the gentlemen's—er—cloakroom, and ten minutes later came back with *thirty-two* pages of the most sensational dialogue.

(GEORGE *enters slowly up* R. *and moves to* L. *of the steps.*)

AUTHOR. But—but I don't even know what's wrong with my twenty pages.

PRODUCER (*gaily*). Everything, my dear sir, just everything.

GEORGE. Excuse me, sir.

PRODUCER. Yes, what is it, George?

GEORGE. You're wanted in the foyer.

PRODUCER. What? (*Irritably.*) No, no. I cannot be interrupted in the middle of rehearsal. Who is it?

GEORGE (*laconically*). A couple of nuns.

PRODUCER (*accepting it*). Oh. (*He realizes what* GEORGE *has said.*) A couple of *what*?

GEORGE. Nuns.

(*The* PRODUCER *is badly shaken.*)

PRODUCER. Really, this is . . . (*He releases the* AUTHOR's *arm and moves down the steps.*) All right, all right, rehearsal dismissed for ten minutes. (*He moves to the bridge and crosses it.*)

(JACKSON *closes his script with a slam, rises, and strides up* L. DAPHNE *rise and moves* L.)

DAPHNE (*following* JACKSON *up* L.). Darling, I suppose you couldn't lend me two pounds ten. . . . ?

(DAPHNE *and* JACKSON *exit up* L.)

PRODUCER (*descending the steps into the auditorium*). A couple of nuns. I ask you.

(*He moves to the stalls door briskly swinging the* AUTHOR's *umbrella, and exits.* GEORGE *studies his stage plan a moment, then looks off* L. *and calls.*)

GEORGE (*calling*). Fred. Just test that safety curtain, will you, mate? (*To the* AUTHOR, *who is still on the rostrum.*) I'm going to put the lights out now, sir.

AUTHOR (*studying his script; vaguely*). Oh, thank you so much.

GEORGE (*moving* L.; *darkly*). Very particular about waste in this theatre, they are.

AUTHOR (*moving down the steps; calling*). Oh—er—excuse me.

(GEORGE *pauses and turns. The safety* CURTAIN *begins to descend.*)

Could you direct me to the gentlemen's—er—cloakroom?

GEORGE *stares at the* AUTHOR *for a moment, then nods and indicates the way off* L. *As they exit* L. *the safety* CURTAIN *reaches the stage and the house-lights come up.*

C

ACT II

As the safety Curtain *is raised the house-lights go out and the stage lights come on. A plain wood form has been set below the table. The stage is empty. After a pause the voices of* Sandra Layton *and* Norwood Beverley *are heard off* R. *raised in argument. After a few moments they enter up* R. Sandra *is a dark "Leading Lady" type of about thirty, smartly dressed and well groomed. She is very pale, obviously tired and living on her nerves.* Norwood *is a good-looking tall man of thirty-five or so, just beginning to show signs of grossness. He wears a good, well-made suit, but it is sadly in need of pressing. His shirt and collar are definitely "off-white" and his tie almost a rag. His shoes have not had a good cleaning for over a week, and the darkness of his unshaven chin accentuates the pallor of his face. There are shadows under his eyes. A rather greasy trilby is stuck at the back of his head.*

Norwood (*moving down* R.; *breathlessly*). Well, I'm damned!

Sandra (*moving* C.). Where are they all?

Norwood (*turning on* Sandra; *very irritated*). I told you that blasted clock in the bedroom was half an hour fast!

Sandra (*moving above the table*). Norwood, please don't be so irritating. I told you before we left the digs that I heard the nine o'clock pips on the landlady's wireless and checked the clock—it was exactly one minute slow. (*She takes a compact from her handbag and powders her nose.*)

Norwood. I didn't hear the pips or see you check the clock.

Sandra. Of course you didn't. You were snoring your head off at the time.

Norwood (*putting his hand to his head*). God! I feel like death.

Sandra. You certainly look the part.

Norwood. My dear Sandra, I am in no mood to listen to your scintillating wit this morning.

Sandra (*shortly*). Sorry.

Norwood (*equally shortly*). Granted. (*He crosses to* L. *and peers off.*) Well, where the devil is everybody? (*He takes a cigarette-case from his pocket, extracts a cigarette and lights it.*)

Sandra. Perhaps they're rehearsing in the dress circle bar.

Norwood. Yes? Look, I may have been on the beer last night and my eyes may be a little dim in consequence, but I can at least see that they've been rehearsing on the stage this morning

Use your brains, woman. The stage is set. (*He perches himself on the* L. *end of the table with his back to* SANDRA.)

SANDRA (*replacing her compact in her bag*). Then why aren't they rehearsing on it now?

NORWOOD. Not being clairvoyant, my dear Sandra, I am unable to enlighten you.

SANDRA (*moving* C.; *controlling her temper, but speaking through her teeth*). Norwood, forgive my mentioning it, but I am getting just a *little* tired of that patronising "My dear Sandra," of yours.

NORWOOD. Are you really?

SANDRA. Yes, dear, a little. I hope that doesn't hurt your pride because, of course, I do know how you've worked on it. You've gurgled it in your bath, you've slobbered it over your beer. You've obviously rehearsed every inflection to the decimal point of a semi-tone, and the timing is perfection, but even perfection palls if you have to spend your life with it.

NORWOOD (*after a slight pause*). Damn you!

SANDRA (*laughing slightly*). Ah, that hurt, didn't it, Norwood? And, of course, no one, not even his wife, has the right to hurt Norwood Beverley, leading man of the popular repertory company, and generally acknowledged as God's gift to Drossmouth.

NORWOOD (*rising; angrily*). Go on. Go on. Sneer. I may be only "God's gift to Drossmouth", but I *have* played in London, my girl, which is more than you ever have—or ever will, I fear. (*He pauses.*) Yes, by God, my name would have been in lights—if it hadn't been for the electricity cut. (*He resumes his seat on the table.*)

SANDRA. Oh, yes, Norwood, you played in London, but—you didn't stay there. You just couldn't make the grade.

NORWOOD (*bitterly and cruelly*). No—I married instead.

(*There is a pause.*)

SANDRA (*turning and moving up* C.; *really hurt*). Norwood—I think that's just about the cruellest, the most unfair thing you've ever said to me.

NORWOOD (*rising quickly and breaking down* L.). Oh, for God's sake shut up. *Shut up.* How the devil d'you expect me to rehearse after you've worn me to a shred with your nattering?

(*Unseen by* SANDRA *and* NORWOOD, MAUD *enters up* R. *She hears nearly all of* NORWOOD's *last speech, but she speaks quietly and placidly.*)

MAUD (*moving* C.). Hallo, dears.

(NORWOOD *and* SANDRA *turn quickly and register relief on seeing it is only* MAUD.)

SANDRA. Hallo, Maudie, my pet.

NORWOOD (*ungraciously*). Hallo.

MAUD. There's a letter for you in the rack, Norwood.

Norwood (*crossing below the steps to* R.). Thanks, I'll get it.

(*He exits up* R.)

Sandra (*with assumed brightness*). How's the rehearsal going, Maudie?

Maud. "Going"? It's almost gone.

Sandra. What *do* you mean? How far have they got? Up to my entrance?

Maud. Don't make me laugh. They're still on page one.

Sandra. Page *one*? What on earth have you been doing all the morning?

Maud. I wouldn't spoil it by telling you. (*She moves to* Sandra.) Sandra, is Norwood being a bit—difficult this morning?

Sandra. Yes, darling, I'm afraid he is—a bit.

Maud (*genuinely*). I'm so sorry. And you have a long part to learn this week, haven't you?

Sandra (*flicking over the pages of her script*). 'Fraid so.

Maud (*with a quick look off* R.). Well, my dear, I know how difficult it is for you when Norwood's—upset. I have to go out this afternoon. You're quite welcome to use my sitting-room— I'll leave a nice fire for you.

Sandra (*kissing* Maud; *with feeling*). Maudie, you are a darling.

(Norwood *enters up* R. *quickly. He is reading a letter.*)

Norwood (*somewhat excited*). Sandra. Sandra. I've had a letter from George Mathews. He's offering me the job of leading man in a new "Rep" he's starting in Blackpool.

Sandra (*not quite knowing what to say*). Oh!

(*There is a pause.*)

Maud. Oh! Very bracing—Blackpool. (*She smiles at* Norwood.)

(Norwood *looks at her stonily.*)

(*She turns and moves hastily to the french window.*) Now where did I leave my script?

(*She exits through the french window.*)

Norwood (*looking sheepishly at* Sandra). I wonder if he's fixed his leading lady yet?

Sandra. I don't think he'd want me, darling. I'm not his type.

Norwood (*moving* R.; *shrugging his shoulders and shoving the letter in his pocket*). Oh, well. It's nice to get these offers, anyway. (*He pauses with his back to* Sandra.) He's offering a damn good salary.

Sandra (*quietly*). If you want to accept it, Norwood . . .

Norwood (*snapping*). I haven't said I want to accept it, have I?

Sandra. No, darling, but . . .

Norwood (*sitting in the chair down* R.; *tersely*). In any case, he's given me a week to think it over.

(JACKSON *enters down* L. *He has his watch in his hands. He crosses to* L. *of* NORWOOD.)

JACKSON. Of course this is fantastic. (*In the same breath.*) 'Morning, Sandra. 'Morning, Norwood. All hell's a-popping here today.

SANDRA. So I gathered.

JACKSON (*holding out his watch*). Look at the time. And we haven't done a stroke yet. Where the devil is Harry? (*He moves to the prompt table and puts the watch on it.*)

(MAUD, *carrying her script, enters through the french window, moves to the chair* L. *of the table and sits.*)

MAUD. Probably romping round the town with his nuns.

SANDRA. His *what?*

MAUD. My dear, that's only the half of it. (*With terrific glee, almost hugging herself.*) Wait and see, darling, just wait and see.

JACKSON. I'll beat the gong. That ought to bring him in.

(*He crosses and exits down* L., *re-entering almost immediately carrying a gong stick and a large gong which he beats vigorously. The noise is terrific.*)

MAUD (*covering her ears and yelling in protest*). Must you, darling, must you?

(*The* PRODUCER *rushes in at the stalls door and comes to the orchestra rail.*)

PRODUCER (*yelling*). All right. All right. I'm here. I'll be with you in a minute. (*As he rushes out again.*) Carry on. Just carry on.

(*He exits through the stalls door.* JACKSON *stops ringing the gong.*)

JACKSON. "Carry on"? What the hell's he mean—"Carry on"? What with?

SANDRA. From where you left off in the play, I suppose.

JACKSON. But dammit. We left off with him telling the author to rewrite the first twenty pages. How the hell d'you carry on from there? (*He strides down* L. *and hurls the gong and beater off* L. *where it lands with a crash.*)

SANDRA (*sitting in the chair above the table*). Maudie, you old devil, you've got to tell me. *What* has been going on here this morning?

(MAUD *whispers to* SANDRA. NORWOOD *takes the letter from his pocket and re-reads it.* JACKSON *sits at the prompt table.*)

DAPHNE (*off up* R.; *calling*). Coming, coming.

AVIS (*off up* R.; *calling*). Sorry, are we on?

(DAPHNE *and* AVIS *enter hurriedly up* R.)

DAPHNE (*moving* L. *of the steps*). Have we begun again?

(AVIS *moves* R. *of the steps.*)

JACKSON (*furiously and derisively*). Have we hell.

DAPHNE (*sitting on the steps*). Oh, we thought we heard the gong.

SANDRA (*calling to* NORWOOD). Norwood. You *must* come and hear all this.

(NORWOOD *rises and crosses to* L. *of* SANDRA *and listens to* MAUD *who is still whispering to* SANDRA. AVIS *sits in the chair that* NORWOOD *has just vacated, takes her letter out and re-reads it.*)

DAPHNE (*looking at her script*). I call that a shame. I've just got the iron nice and hot. I've got three weeks' laundry hanging in the dressing-room just yearning to be ironed. (*She looks around.*) I say, where's our tame author? Has he left the country?

(JERRY *enters up* R. *and moves* C.)

JERRY. I say, Jacko. What's wrong with the door of the "gents" upstairs?

JACKSON (*rising and crossing to* JERRY *slowly; this is the last straw*). Listen, old boy. I am the stage director in this theatre, *not* the ruddy lavatory attendant.

JERRY. All right, old man. Don't get your hair off. I only asked because I've been trying to get in there for the last quarter of an hour . . .

DAPHNE (*with mock modesty*). Per-lease.

JERRY. But the door won't open. (*He moves up* R.) I mean, it's so awkward, isn't it?

(*He exits up* R. MARY, *holding a large hideous lampshade aloft, enters down* L.)

JACKSON (*unable to forgive or forget the insult; to himself*). Of all the darned sauce. (*He turns and sees* MARY *holding the lampshade aloft.*) What are you standing there holding that thing up for?

MARY (*almost lost behind the shade*). I want to ask Mr Blacker what's wrong with it.

JACKSON (*with an almost hysterical whine*). Well, *don't* stand there holding the thing up like that. For goodness sake put it down somewhere. With everything going so darned crazy in this theatre this morning, you'll be turning into a standard lamp before you know where you are.

(*There is a burst of laughter from* MAUD, SANDRA *and* NORWOOD.)

Oh, shut up.

(*They take no notice of* JACKSON *and the laughter continues.* MARY *turns and exits with the lampshade down* L.)

(*Wearily.*) Oh, God! (*He moves down* L. *shouting to* MARY.) Mary, I'm going up to my office for a bottle of Aspirin.

(*He exits down* L. DAPHNE *looks through her script.*)

DAPHNE (*not too worried about it*). Well, if he's going to cut that first scene with the butler, there's nothing left in my part but two "No, madam's", three "Yes, madam's" and an exit. Never mind, we'll press on.

SANDRA (*calling to* AVIS). Oh, Avis, did you remember to ask Mrs . . . ?

(AVIS *rises hurriedly and exits quickly off* R., *obviously again on the verge of tears.*)

What's the matter with Avis?

DAPHNE. She's upset, poor kid. Got to give up the stage, go home and run the vicarage for her father, and marry the curate.

SANDRA. Oh, I *see*. She's crying for joy.

(*The* PRODUCER *enters through the stalls door.*)

PRODUCER (*all out for business*). Now, come along. Come along, everyone. What's going on? Why aren't you rehearsing? (*He is down by the orchestra rail.*)

MAUD. We've been waiting for you, dear.

PRODUCER. Oh. I—er—had to slip across and see my book-maker. I had a very good tip for the three-thirty.

SANDRA. Not from the nuns, surely?

PRODUCER (*laughing*). No, not from the nuns. Everybody on stage, please.

(MARY *enters down* L., *still holding the lampshade aloft.*)

Mary darling. Unwind yourself out of that lampshade and sound the gong, will you?

(MARY *turns and exits hurriedly* L. *The sound of the gong is heard.*)

No, it was funny about those nuns. They want us . . . (*He yells.*) All right, that's enough, Mary.

(*The gong stops.*)

MAUD. What were you saying, dear?

PRODUCER. The nuns. They want one of you girls to go up to the convent and produce the children in a Nativity play. How about it, Maudie?

MAUD (*heavily*). Well, as I said before, dear, I'll try anything once.

PRODUCER (*moving up the steps and over the bridge*). Good for you. (*He moves* C.) Now, please, *please*. We *must* get on. Where's Jacko? Have I a stage director, or have I not.

(JACKSON, *carrying a glass of water and a bottle of Aspirin tablets, enters up* L. *and moves to the prompt table.*)

JACKSON. You won't have this one in a fortnight's time. (*He takes an Aspirin and puts the glass and bottle on the prompt table.*)

PRODUCER (*moving to* JACKSON; *like a disappointed schoolboy*). Oh, Jacko, you're not going to give your notice in again, are you?

(MARY *enters down* L. *and sits on the floor below the prompt table*.)

JACKSON. If I don't get out of this crazy fun factory soon, I'll go mad. I'm used to working with producers who know what they want, when they want it, and how to get it.

PRODUCER (*quietly—but with no menace*). Jacko, you're not casting aspersions on my methods of production, are you?

JACKSON. I can't. I've never seen 'em.

PRODUCER (*with dignity*). Jacko—we will talk this over quietly and, I hope, with dignity, later on. (*He shouts.*) *Now. Can we get on?* (*He crosses to his corner down* R.)

NORWOOD (*moving* C.). Don't shout like that, old boy. I've got a hell of a head this morning, and I've had no breakfast.

(JACKSON *sits at the prompt table*.)

SANDRA (*not cattily*). Darling, you've no-one but yourself to blame for that.

NORWOOD (*almost shouting*). Well, for God's sake don't jump down my throat every time I open my mouth. (*He picks up the chair* R. *of the table and moves it, preparatory to sitting by himself*.)

JACKSON. Half a minute, old boy, half a minute. That chair's on the set. What d'you think you're playing at.

NORWOOD (*slamming the chair back into position*). Oh, for Heaven's sake. I'll be in my dressing-room when I'm wanted.

(*As he is striding off up* R. *he collides with the* AUTHOR *who enters up* R. *at that moment*.)

(*Witheringly.*) That's right. Kill my exit.

(*He exits up* R. *The* AUTHOR, *studying some notes he is carrying, wanders to the chair* R. *of the table and sits*.)

PRODUCER (*seeing the* AUTHOR). Who's that?

JACKSON (*hissing*). It's the author.

PRODUCER (*moving to the* AUTHOR *and speaking as if greeting a dear old friend of many years standing, after a long absence*). My dear old boy. How nice to see you again. Where have you been?

AUTHOR (*nervously rising*). In the—I—that is . . .

PRODUCER. We missed you.

AUTHOR. Mr Blacker, I—(*he produces a sheet of paper on which is written a small number of words*)—I've started re-writing the first twenty pages, as you suggested. I'm afraid I haven't done very much, but (*proffering the paper*) if you think this is proceeding along the right lines.

PRODUCER (*taking the paper and obviously not reading it; ecstatically*). That's excellent, my dear sir, excellent. Just what we wanted. (*He rubs his hands together enthusiastically moving down* R. *In doing this he screws the paper into a ball, which he hurls into the orchestra well.)* Now, we'll put in some really hard work, shall we. (*He marches* C. *singing with great abandon.*) "Hi-diddle-di-dee. An actor's life for me." (*From "Pinocchio."*) Off we go. (*He shoos the* AUTHOR *off* L.) Off we go. (*He turns and crosses down* R.)

(JERRY *enters up* R.)

JACKSON (*in a dead voice*). What with?
PRODUCER (*still happily*). Hmm?
JACKSON (*in the same voice*). What are you starting with?
PRODUCER (*innocently*). Act One, of course.

(*The* AUTHOR *enters down* L.)

JACKSON. But dammit. Half of it isn't written yet. Haven't you just told that poor devil . . .
PRODUCER (*reprovingly*). Jacko. Jacko. (*With dignity.*) *Toujours La Petite Gentilhomme.*
JACKSON (*wearily*). Harry, it is now eleven-fifteen. . . .
PRODUCER. Eleven-fifteen? Then why haven't we had coffee? Mary, go and get the coffee.

(MARY *rises and moves to the* PRODUCER.)

You will all have it on me this morning. And, Mary, get me an ounce of Three Nuns—(*quickly*)—no—Four Square tobacco at the same time. (*He takes some coins from his pocket and counts them.*)
MARY (*holding out her hand for the money*). Yes, Mr Blacker.
PRODUCER (*replacing the coins in his pocket*). And tell Mrs Thing to put it down to my account.
MARY (*without enthusiasm*). Yes, Mr Blacker.

(*She turns and exits up* L.)

PRODUCER. We'll do some more work while we're waiting for the coffee to arrive. We'll do some of Act Two. Come along everybody. (*He moves to his corner down* R.)

(*There is a general movement from the company.* JERRY *lies down on the form up* C. SANDRA *stands above the table.* DAPHNE *crosses to the chair up* L. *and sits. The* AUTHOR *is hovering down* L. JACKSON *is seated at the prompt table.*)

MAUD (*rising quickly*). That's us, Sandra. Now let me see. (*She refers to her script.*) Oh, yes. I'm sitting in the easy chair by the fire. (*She crosses to the chair down* R. *and sits.*)
JACKSON. Right. Stand by. Clear stage, everybody.
AUTHOR (*almost out of sight; nervously to* JACKSON). Am I in the way here?
JACKSON (*ignoring him*). Curtain up.
MAUD (*reading her part*). "Geoffrey is late home tonight, Melisande."

SANDRA (*reading her part*). "Geoffrey always seems to be late home these days, Mother."

MAUD (*reading*). "There's nothing wrong between you and Geoffrey, is there, Melisande?"

SANDRA (*reading*). "Wrong? No, of course not, Mother dear. Why should there be?"

MAUD (*reading*). "I don't know. I just asked, Melisande."

PRODUCER (*irritably*). Oh, not again, surely.

MAUD. What?

PRODUCER. The curtain has only been up precisely two seconds and you've already said that damned name Melisande three times.

MAUD. Well, darling, they're in the script.

PRODUCER. Well, cut them out. *Two* of them, anyway.

MAUD. Which two?

PRODUCER (*heavily*). Does it matter? Toss for it! Carry on.

SANDRA (*reading*). "You wouldn't ask if there was anything wrong, unless you had a reason, Mother."

MAUD (*reading*). "No, no reason, Melis . . ." (*After a quick glance at the* PRODUCER.) I suppose that had better come out, too. (*Then as if she had had a wonderful idea.*) Oh. Shall I say *dear*, instead?

PRODUCER (*after thought*). It's a very nice old Anglo-Saxon word.

MAUD (*reading*). "No, no reason, dear! But I had felt that perhaps—but maybe I am wrong."

SANDRA (*reading*). "What have you felt, Mother?"

MAUD (*reading*). "Nothing, dear, only . . ."

SANDRA (*reading*). "Only what?"

MAUD (*reading*). "It's only my foolish fancy."

SANDRA (*reading*). "What is?"

MAUD (*reading*). "Oh, nothing, dear."

PRODUCER (*with a strangled yell*). No. No. No. (*In an agony of torment he moves* C., *hands clutched together and body swaying with misery.*) It's all quibbling, quibbling, quibbling. Splitting hairs. Don't you see? Either the bloody woman *knows* there's something wrong or she doesn't. And if she *does* then for God's sake let her say so in *one line*, and not go nattering on about "Nothing, dear," "Nothing, dear." (*It is too much for him. He produces a handkerchief and moves sobbing to the* R. *proscenium.*) Ooooooh!

(*Everyone watches him.*)

(*At last he turns, wiping away the tears from both eyes, then speaks in a quavering whimper.*) People shouldn't be allowed to write plays. (*He pulls himself together.*) Now, come along, we really must get this straightened out. (*He crosses to the* AUTHOR.) I'm *not* being difficult, old boy, and you *do* see my point, don't you? (*He drags the* AUTHOR *to* C.) Now just a little co-operation and we'll get this thing right in no time. We'll work on it together. (*Then a sudden thought strikes him—he speaks almost in horror.*) My dear *sir*. You haven't met everybody, have you? I haven't introduced you. My dear old boy, you must forgive me! (*To the company.*) Everybody, please. This is the Author, Mr—er—er—who has most kindly come along today to clear up the finer points of his lovely, lovely play. Ladies and gentlemen, the Author. (*He almost waits for the "round" of applause—which does not come—and he repeats more loudly.*) *The author. Everybody.*

(DAPHNE *applauds feebly.*)

That's right. Now let's begin the act again, shall we? (*He moves down* R. *taking the* AUTHOR *with him.*) You come and stand over here with me, old boy, and help me clear up any knotty little problems that might arise. All right, Maudie, let it *rip*.

MAUD (*reading*). "Geoffrey is late home tonight—(*with a quick look at the* PRODUCER, *then slipping it in quickly*)—Melisande."

PRODUCER. Lovely, darling.

SANDRA (*reading*). "Geoffrey always seems to be late home these days, Mother."

MAUD (*reading*). "There's nothing wrong between you and . . ."

PRODUCER (*interrupting*). Just a moment, dear. (*He leads the* AUTHOR *up* C. *to* R. *of where* SANDRA *is standing.*) Sandra, we— (*meaning the* AUTHOR *and himself*)—don't quite like you standing behind that table all the time. We certainly don't want you standing there when the curtain goes up, do *we*, old boy?

SANDRA (*reading*). "She is standing behind the table as the curtain rises." (*To the* PRODUCER.) It's in the script.

PRODUCER (*grandly*). In the *script*—yes. But, surely, darling, we can improve on *that*? No. I see you standing . . .(*He is about to indicate exactly where the* AUTHOR *is standing; slightly impatiently, moving the* AUTHOR *to* L.) Just "Clear" a moment, old boy, will you, please.

(*The* AUTHOR *moves unhappily to his original position down* L.)

(*He moves* SANDRA *to* L. *of the steps; ecstatically.*) Yes, that's it. The curtain goes up and Maud is sitting in the fire, gazing at the easy chair. (*He corrects himself.*) No, sitting in the easy chair gazing at the fire. And you, darling, are standing here—(*he moves her to exactly the right position*)—looking your loveliest in a beautifully cut black evening gown which shows off the lines of your body to perfection. That will make a perfect picture. (*He backs below the table.*)

SANDRA (*very practically*). And where's it coming from?

PRODUCER (*blithely*). What, dear?

SANDRA. The beautifully cut black evening gown that shows off the lines of my body, etc., etc. Are the *management* going to provide it?

PRODUCER (*quite sure on this point*). Oh no, darling. I'm afraid we can't ask the management to . . .

SANDRA (*interrupting*). You mean I've got to find it?

PRODUCER (*with an eloquent shrug of the shoulders*). Well, darling. . . .

SANDRA (*putting her script on the table*). Do you know how many changes of dress I have in this play?

PRODUCER. No, dear.

SANDRA. I'll enlighten you. For my first entrance I sweep down the stairs in a delightful négligée.

(*The* AUTHOR, *burrowing in his script to settle the question of* SANDRA'S *dresses, approaches the* PRODUCER, *who has his back to him.* SANDRA *and the* PRODUCER *begin moving casually down towards the prompt table as they speak. The* AUTHOR *is borne along with them unconsciously.*)

I'm on the stage exactly three minutes before I rush upstairs again to reappear five minutes later in an "obviously beautifully tailored two-piece". I stand on the top of the stairs for one second and as I begin to descend—the curtain falls.

(*They crush the* AUTHOR *up against the prompt table and he sits on it.* JACKSON *removes the glass of water in the nick of time.*)

(*She moves below the table and picks up her script.*) Nice expensive little start-off, isn't it?

PRODUCER (*moving to her; patiently*). In Repertory, darling, you must *expect* to have to . . .

SANDRA (*firmly*). I do *not* expect to have to find three négligeés, three evening gowns, two "tailor-mades" and a Chinchilla coat —which is what this part demands.

(*The* AUTHOR *rises from the prompt table and moves down* L. JACKSON *retrieves his watch which the* AUTHOR *has been sitting on and shakes it to see if it still works.*)

PRODUCER (*slightly shaken*). Hmm! I see your point. Never mind, we'll talk it over after rehearsal, shall we?

SANDRA. We most certainly will.

PRODUCER. Bless you, darling. (*He kisses* SANDRA.) I knew you'd be reasonable.

(*There is the sound of a loud male snore from* JERRY.)

(*After a pause, glaring at the* AUTHOR.) Did you do that?

MAUD. It's Jerry, darling. (*She points to where* JERRY *is stretched out asleep on the wooden form.*) He's fast asleep.

JACKSON (*grimly*). He's lucky.

(*Another snore from* JERRY. *The* AUTHOR *wanders off down* L.)

PRODUCER (*striding down to the* R. *proscenium*). How *dare* he? How dare *anyone* fall asleep during one of *my* rehearsals. *This is the end.*

(*Another even louder snore from* JERRY.)

DAPHNE (*rising*). Shall I wake him up, Mr Blacker?

PRODUCER (*thundering*). You will stay where you are, young woman. Who are *we* to disturb Mr Jerry Winterton's slumbers?

(*Another enormous snore from* JERRY. DAPHNE *resumes her seat.*)

(*Very pained.*) Irving wouldn't have stood for this.

(JERRY *snores again.*)

I repeat, Irving would *not* have stood for this.

JACKSON (*leaping to his feet*). Then why the hell do *you?*

PRODUCER (*more pained than ever*). Jacko, *please.*

JACKSON (*livid*). "Jacko, please," be damned. You're enjoying this, aren't you? You're loving it. It's giving you an opening for another scene. Instead of getting on with the rehearsal, we all have to sit round and watch you put on another one of your bloody acts. What's it supposed to be this time? The wounded doe? Do you realize what time it is? Do you know how much rehearsing we've done so far? We haven't got through one full page of dialogue. All we've done is watch you acting yourself sick. What *are* we? A repertory company or the Harry Blacker admiration society?

(*There is a pause. The* PRODUCER *stands motionless by the proscenium, his hands well in his pockets. He holds this pose for a time, then slowly crosses to* JACKSON.)

PRODUCER (*reminiscently*). I remember once, I was rehearsing for a new play called—er—*Baffled Bedfellows.* Gerald du Maurier was producing. At one rehearsal the stage director presumed to address Sir Gerald in the same sordid way that Jacko has just presumed to address me. Du Maurier was amazing. He did not so much as flicker an eyelash!

JACKSON (*after a pause*). All right. I'll buy it. What *did* he do?

PRODUCER. Merely struck the man dead at his feet. (*He moves to his position down* R.) But we were a very loyal company, so it never came out at the inquest. Just—heart failure.

(*There is a pause.*)

MAUD (*rising*). Look, Harry, I don't mind bedtime stories at bedtime, but not at this time of the morning.

(MARY *enters up* R. *carrying a tray with six cups of coffee on it. She puts the tray on the little rostrum at the top of the steps* R.C.)

MARY. Coffee, everyone.

(*The company break for coffee.* JACKSON *moves to the prompt table and looks through some of his papers.* MAUD *takes a cup of coffee, puts her script on the mantelpiece, and exits up* R. MARY *picks up two cups, hands one to the* PRODUCER, *then exits up* R. *The* PRODUCER *exits with his cup down* R. DAPHNE *rises and moves to the steps, slapping* JERRY *as she passes him.*)

DAPHNE. Wake up, Jerry, coffee. (*She picks up a cup of coffee and eases up* R.)

JERRY (*waking in a flurry and sitting up*). Where am I? (*He realizes.*) Oh, hell! Rehearsal. And I was having such a lovely dream, too. I dreamed that I'd just been offered the lead in a new Noel Coward musical.

SANDRA (*picking up a cup of coffee; pleasantly sarcastic*). Did you accept it, dear? (*She crosses up* L.)

JERRY (*rising*). No. They got Donald Wolfit instead. (*He picks up the last cup of coffee.*)

(SANDRA *exits up* L. DAPHNE *and* JERRY *exit up* R. JACKSON *rises and moves* C. *As he does so, the* PRODUCER *enters down* R. *and also moves* C. *They meet* C. *and for a second stare at each other, then* JACKSON *moves below the* PRODUCER *to the steps and reaches for a cup of coffee, but it has all been taken.* JACKSON, *furious, catches the* PRODUCER'S *eye. The* PRODUCER *chuckles nastily.* JACKSON *exits angrily up* R. *The* PRODUCER, *his cup of coffee in his hand, moves on to the bridge and addresses the audience in conversational tones—as one man to another.*)

PRODUCER. Well—how are you little lot getting on? Enjoying yourselves? (*He drinks some coffee.*) I'm sorry I can't offer you any of this, I'm afraid there wouldn't be enough to go round. I'll bet you're just sitting there wondering what the devil this is all about. But then, I dare say, if I came along to your businesses, your offices or your factories, or what have you, and sat in a corner for half an hour or so, I should be just as mystified as you are now. Actually, you know, a repertory theatre isn't unlike a factory—in fact, we often call it the fun factory. In a factory you turn out so much of whatever commodity it is you make a week. In this theatre, we turn out a play a week. And so it goes on, week after week, fifty-two weeks a year. (*With sudden alarm.*) Oh, I say. *Please* don't think I'm asking you to be sorry for us. I should hate you to think that. But, you know, people who don't know anything about the theatre, do have the most amazing ideas. I've known people to be quite staggered when they've heard that actors have to *learn* their parts. "Oh, do they?" they say, "I thought they made them up as they went along." (*He laughs pleasantly and sips his coffee.*) One thing, thank God—we're a very happy little company here. No temperaments or anything like that. But you'll have seen that for yourselves. (*He pauses.*) What's

the matter? What are you laughing at? Oh, I get it. You're thinking about Jacko's little outburst just now. You mustn't take any
notice of *that*. We expect Jacko to give in his notice at least twice
daily. Once just before we break for morning coffee, and half-
way through Act Two at night. Mind you, I'm not saying that——

(Avis, *unhappy and nervous, enters down* R. *carrying her letter.*)

Avis Producer	(*together*).	Mr Blacker . . . —I don't fly off the handle some-times, but——
Avis Producer	(*together; louder*).	Mr Blacker . . . —if you could . . .

(*The* Producer *realizes someone is behind him and turns.*)

Avis. Mr Blacker . . .
Producer. Good Lord! (*He moves on to the stage.*) What is it,
child? What is it?
Avis (*somewhat mystified*). I'm sorry if I interrupted you. Were
you—you *talking* to someone?
Producer (*a bit flustered*). No, no. I was just—er—rehearsing
a speech I used to . . . What do you want?
Avis. Mr Blacker, I wanted to tell you that . . .
Producer. My dear Avis, let *me* tell *you* something first. You'll
never be a tragedy queen unless you learn to hold yourself like
one. How many times have I told you to be careful of your deport-
ment.

(Maud *enters up* R., *carrying a jug of coffee and her cup, which she refills.
She has her handbag under her arm.*)

Look at the way you're standing now, like a sack of coal. (*He
braces her shoulders back.*) Hold yourself up, child. (*He pushes her
tummy in.*) Get rid of that, and—(*he pushes her posterior with the other
hand*)—do something about that.
Maud (*putting the jug on the tray*). Now, Harry, don't be unkind.
(*She puts her handbag on the steps.*)
Producer. Oh, Maudie, I didn't see you there. Darling, just
teach this child how to move—how to stand—will you? (*He moves
to the bridge.*) I've got to go over to the post office and get a three
and sixpenny postal order for my Pools. (*He quickly crosses the
bridge, descends the steps and moves to the stalls door.*)
Avis (*calling after him*). But, Mr Blacker . . .
Producer. Don't worry, Avis, we'll make an actress of you yet.

(*He exits breezily through the stalls door.* Avis *looks extremely near to
tears.*)

Maud. Cheer up, Avis. Surely you know Harry well enough not
to be upset by his nonsense?

AVIS. But he wouldn't listen to me. I wanted to tell him that I've got to give in my notice. I've got to go home.

MAUD. Oh, yes, of course. Daphne did say something about that. You're going to marry the curate, aren't you? Darling, I'm so happy for you.

(AVIS *begins to sob*.)

(*Mystified*.) Avis.

AVIS. I don't want to go home. I don't want to give up the stage. But I've got to look after father. He needs me.

MAUD. Trust Daphne to get hold of the wrong end of the stick. But, Avis, if your father needs you, you must go. And, after all, life on the stage can be just one long heart-breaking struggle.

AVIS. But I was prepared for that. I wouldn't have minded how hard I worked, or how long, if only one day I could have got right to the top.

MAUD. Well, hard work may make you a competent actress, but it'll never make you into a great one—unless you've got the —the spark of genius in you, and—can I be quite frank with you?

AVIS. Of course, Maudie.

MAUD. Take a deep breath 'cos it's going to hurt. (*Slowly*.) I don't think you've got that spark.

(*There is a pause*. AVIS *turns away and moves towards the bench below the table*.)

Does that sound very cruel?

AVIS (*turning*). No—only . . . (*She sits on the bench*.)

MAUD. Only what?

AVIS. I was thinking. When you were a girl, starting on the stage like me, you must have decided it was worth it—the struggle, I mean.

MAUD. Oh, but I was born in the business. I didn't have to decide anything. I was first carried on when I was six months old —and I've never stopped acting since. (*She moves to* R. *of* AVIS.) I played every kind of part from the time I was sixteen, and my salary was twenty-five shillings a week—until I got my first "leading lady" part—then it went down to twenty-two.

AVIS. But you couldn't live on that.

MAUD. I had to live on it.

AVIS. How awful. But they've got to pay you a decent living wage nowadays. Things have changed.

MAUD. They have indeed. Anyway, take my advice for what it's worth. If your father wants you to go home, then go—and find a nice husband for yourself and forget all about this acting non-sense.

(*She moves to the tray on the rostrum and puts down her cup*.)

AVIS. Couldn't I do both? I mean—act *and* find a nice husband? After all, you did, didn't you?

MAUD (*turning*). Eh? Yes, I did—dear old John, bless him. (*She moves a little towards* AVIS.) He was my first leading man. We spent so much time on the stage locked in each other's arms and vowing eternal love I suppose it was only natural we should find ourselves doing it off stage, too. Propinquity had something to do with it—though, of course, I didn't know the meaning of the word in those days. Anyway, we married.

AVIS. Oh, then weren't you really in love?

MAUD. Yes, I was in love. (*She sits* R. *of* AVIS *on the bench.*) And John thought a lot of me as an actress, too. He even wrote a play for me. It was called *Her Faith Against the World*.

AVIS. *Her Faith* . . .

MAUD (*laughing*). Silly title, wasn't it?

AVIS. Did it ever get produced?

MAUD. Oh, yes. We did it ourselves, when we'd saved up enough money. We toured it for two years. We went round and round until one day I said to John, "Look here, if we don't stop going round and round like this, I shall get giddy."

AVIS. What did he say to that?

MAUD. Something rather surprising. He said, "Next stop London for you, my girl," and he meant it, too. You see, we'd made quite a lot of money with the old *Faith* by that time.

AVIS (*absorbed*). Well? What happened to it?

MAUD (*slowly*). Well, the play wasn't really very good and nobody in London had ever heard of me—so there was nothing to pull them in at the box office. John ran it as long as the money lasted. He kept hoping that business would pick up because the notices had been so good. (*She pauses.*) At least, they were wonderful to me.

AVIS. You must have been thrilled.

MAUD. I think I was more dumbfounded—overawed, after struggling for all those years. John was so happy for me. He couldn't understand why I wanted to cry. (*She is indeed close to tears now.*)

AVIS (*softly*). Oh, *no*.

MAUD. No? (*She rises quickly and moves to the steps.*) Why am I telling you all this? (*She takes a handkerchief from her bag.*)

AVIS. Oh, you must go on, Maudie. I'd no idea you'd been a star.

MAUD. I find it difficult to believe myself sometimes; but when I'm feeling down and thinking, "Maud, you're no good, and you never have been", I get the old press cuttings out and read them over. It cheers me up. I've got them here; always carry them about with me—just in case. (*She pauses. Rather wistfully.*) Like to see them?

AVIS (*rising and crossing to* MAUD). Yes, please.

MAUD (*taking some cuttings from her bag*). Unforgivable sin, showing people old press notices—almost as bad as snapshots.

D

And as for reading them yourself . . . But I only do it when I'm
very down. (*She hands the cuttings to* AVIS, *then sits on the steps.*)

AVIS (*reading*). "Triumph for new young actress." . . . "Actress
with a great heart." (*She returns the cuttings to* MAUD.)

MAUD (*after a pause*). Yes. I suppose the trouble was I hadn't
got enough head. (*She replaces the cuttings in her bag.*)

AVIS. But you must have had masses of offers when the play
closed. (*She sits on the steps up stage of* MAUD.)

MAUD. Well, managers said it was a question of "getting the
right part". The right part always seemed to be round the corner,
but I could never catch up with it. Still I *did* hold out—for six
awful months. Meantime, John got a job on tour, so he was all
right. It was the first time that we'd been parted since we were
married and we both felt awful about it, and then—well, John
had more love scenes to play and the old "propinquity" did its
stuff again.

AVIS (*incredulous*). You mean he was unfaithful to you?

MAUD (*quietly*). She was a pretty little thing.

AVIS. But after all you'd been through together . . .

MAUD. One has to try and be sensible about that sort of thing,
but I can't pretend it helped at the time.

AVIS. But it wasn't serious, was it?

MAUD. It certainly seemed so then. It broke me up for a bit,
but it all straightened out in the end. I think John had somehow
got the idea that he was standing in my way—that I'd be better
on my own. But I soon got all that nonsense out of his head, and
I put all ideas of stardom out of mine and settled down to domes-
tic bliss touring the country with John. 'Course, we'd plenty of
ups and downs after that, but we were the best of pals to the day
he died.

AVIS. Haven't you any regrets when you look back and think
what you might have done—well—what you *did*?

MAUD. I'll tell you what I try to think. (*She pauses.*) When I
remember to thank God for the gifts he gave me, I say, "I've had
a good life—with a good husband—good health, always some
sort of a roof over my head and enough to eat and drink." Has
anyone the right to ask for more?

AVIS. If I were in your place I'd feel awfully bitter.

MAUD (*softly*). Would you, AVIS? Then that's all the more
reason why you ought to give it up now. (*She holds* AVIS's *head
against her.*) I shouldn't like to think of you ever growing bitter.
So, if you feel you couldn't take the "buffets and rewards with
equal thanks"—that's Shakespeare. Did you know that?

AVIS (*in a very small voice*). No.

MAUD. No. You see. 'Course you didn't—child's an ignoramus.
You go back to your nice warm secure home. You'll thank me
later on. (*She pushes* AVIS *to her feet, then rises and picks up her handbag.*)

(AVIS *stands with her back to* MAUD.)

Though you probably think I'm an awful old "what's-it" now, don't you?

(*There is a pause.*)

Do you?

(Avis *turns and hugs* Maud *and they both move* c.)

And just in case I've given the impression I'm sprouting wings and a halo, I'll tell you something that does get me by the throat sometimes. I sit looking round my landlady's room and think "Maudie, you've been working all your life—ever since you were a child—and you've never had a home—not so much as a stick of furniture you could call your own." (*She pauses, and turns away from* Avis.) But I will have—one day.

Avis (*timidly*). I think it's wonderful how you can still hope.

Maud (*suddenly; almost in tears*). Good Heavens, child—I'm not as old as all that.

(*She exits quickly down* R.)

Avis (*calling after her*). Oh, I didn't mean that. Maudie. Maudie.

(George *enters up* L.)

George. Are you still rehearsing, miss?

Avis. No.

George (*pleased*). Then you don't want all these lights on, do you?

(*He crosses and exits down* L. Avis *moves down* R. *and exits. The* Producer *enters breezily through the stalls door as* Jerry, *studying his script, enters up* R.)

Producer (*as he enters*). Now, come along, everybody, come along. We've got to get some work done. (*He quotes.*) "We've such a lot to do, my love, and so little time to do it in." (*Thoughtfully.*) What play does that come out of?

Jerry (*absently*). Charley's Aunt.

Producer. Thanks. (*He begins to climb the steps to the bridge.*) Now come along, where are they all? Where are they? (*He calls.*) Jacko.

(*As he reaches the bridge the lights on the stage go out.*)

Jerry (*shouting*). Lights. Lights.

Producer. Who's messing about with the lights? Put them on, you damn fool. Do you want me to break my neck? *Help.*

{*The lights go on again and the* Producer *is seen on his hands and knees his back to the audience, clinging to the sides of the bridge, terrified.* Jerry *is standing on the steps* R.C.)

(*Furiously, as he crawls across the bridge to the stage.*) Who did it? Who did it? Where is he? Let me get my hands on him. (*He stands up.*)

(George *enters down* L.)

GEORGE (*unperturbed*). What's up?

PRODUCER (*furiously moving to* GEORGE). Did you put those lights out?

GEORGE. 'Course I did.

PRODUCER (*livid*). You blithering idiot. You blundering fool. You—you very bad stage carpenter. What would have happened if I'd crashed into the orchestra well? Well?

GEORGE (*stolidly*). I ain't no good at quizzes.

PRODUCER. What made you put them out in the first place?

GEORGE (*snapping*). 'Cos I thought rehearsal was over.

PRODUCER (*magnificently*). How dare you think.

GEORGE. Now, calm down. Calm down.

PRODUCER. I will *not* calm down. When I think how near death I was at that moment . . .

(JACKSON *enters down* R.)

JACKSON. What's the matter now?

GEORGE. When I was wiv Martin-'Arvey . . .

(MAUD *enters up* R., *followed by* MARY.)

PRODUCER. Matter? (*He points to* GEORGE.) This—this remnant of the very last tour of *The Only Way* nearly killed me, that's all. Maudie. Where's Maudie?

(MARY *picks up the coffee tray and puts it under the steps* R.C.)

MAUD (*moving to the* PRODUCER). Here I am, darling.

PRODUCER. Maudie, have you any—er—smelling salts in your dressing-room?

MAUD (*smiling*). Darling, if you mean is my brandy flask up there—yes. (*She breaks up* C.)

PRODUCER. Mary.

(MARY *runs to the* PRODUCER.)

Help me to Maudie's room. I think I'm going to die.

(*He puts his right arm around* MARY's *shoulder and they move* L.)

(*As he crosses below* GEORGE. *Witheringly.*) You—get back to your hammer and sickle.

(*The* PRODUCER *and* MARY *exit* L.)

JACKSON (*crossing to* GEORGE). George. What happened?

GEORGE. It weren't my fault. 'Ow was I ter know 'e'd be crossing the bridge when I put the lights out?

(DAPHNE *and* AVIS *enter up* R. *and stand listening.*)

JACKSON (*hopefully*). He didn't fall in the orchestra pit, did he?

(AVIS *whispers to* JERRY.)

GEORGE. 'Course he didn't.

JACKSON (*grimly*). Then why didn't you make sure that he did?

MAUD (*half laughing, half shocked*). Jacko. Jacko.

JACKSON. He isn't hurt, is he?

JERRY (*sitting on the steps*). Of course he isn't. Just scared.

(SANDRA *enters down* R.)

JACKSON (*crossing to* SANDRA). Oh, Sandra. (*He takes a letter in a sealed envelope from his pocket.*) Letter for you. Second post's in. Nothing for anyone else. (*He gives the letter to* SANDRA.)

(SANDRA *sits in the chair down* R., *opens the letter and reads it.*)

(*He moves* C.) I wonder if our worthy producer is going to stay scared long enough for us to get some work done? (*To* GEORGE.) George, if you see Mr Blacker come anywhere near the stage, drop a twenty-eight pound counter-weight on his head.

MAUD. Jacko. You shouldn't say such things, even as a joke.

JACKSON (*grimly*). Who's joking?

GEORGE (*chattily*). We were playing the old Theatre Royal, Huddersfield, once, and the local stage carpenter . . .

JACKSON (*moving to* GEORGE *and taking him by the arm*). Yes, yes, of course. (*He leads* GEORGE *up* R.) Yes, well, we'll go into all that later.

(*He gives him a shove and* GEORGE *exits up* R.)

(*He crosses quickly to the prompt table.*) Come along, everyone, we must get on.

(MAUD *eases above the table.* DAPHNE *moves* R. *of the table.* JERRY *rises and moves above the steps* R.C.)

Stand by, everyone, please. Let's go from where we left off. Maudie—Sandra.

(SANDRA *is absorbed in her letter.*)

(*He calls.*) Sandra.

(SANDRA *still does not respond.*)

(*He calls louder.*) Sandra, darling, do stand by.

SANDRA (*looking up; startled*). What? Oh, yes, I'm so sorry. (*She rises and moves below the steps* R.C.) I think I'm going to faint.

(*Everyone exclaims and all move to* SANDRA. MAUD *moves* R. *of the steps and helps* SANDRA *to sit on them.* JERRY *and* AVIS *move in above the steps.* JACKSON *crosses to* L. *of the steps.* AVIS *eases* L. *of* JACKSON.)

MAUD. Sandra. You haven't had bad news, have you?

SANDRA. Bad news? No, it's wonderful—wonderful—but I— I just can't believe it. I . . . (*She bursts into silent weeping.*)

MAUD Sandra, darling, what . . . ?

SANDRA (*blindly holding out the letter*). Jacko, read this.

(JACKSON *takes the letter and reads it to himself. All eyes are on him except* SANDRA'S.)

JACKSON (*after reading a bit*). God! How marvellous.

MAUD. Well, I'm not an inquisitive person, but . . .

DAPHNE. Well, I *am*—damned inquisitive, and if somebody doesn't read me that letter, I shall go off pop.

JACKSON. Shall I, Sandra?

(*Unseen by any of them* NORWOOD *enters up* L., *carrying his coffee cup and a newspaper.*)

SANDRA. Of course.

JACKSON. It's from the Old Vic Company.

(NORWOOD *looks up interested, but stays in the background.*)

DAPHNE (*in a quavering, agonized voice*). Read it, for Heaven's sake, read it.

JACKSON (*reading*). "Dear Miss Layton."

(NORWOOD *starts, and lowers his newspaper.*)

Sir Laurence Olivier . . .

DAPHNE (*collapsing weakly into the chair* R. *of the table*). Oh— Larry.

JERRY. Oh, shut up. Go on, Jacko.

JACKSON (*reading*). Sir Laurence Olivier, who has recently been staying in Yorkshire, had the pleasure of seeing two productions given by the Drossmouth Repertory Company and was most impressed by the high standard shown by the entire company."

(*Slight reaction of pleasure from all.*)

"He was, however, particularly impressed by the excellence and versatility of your work. On his suggestion I am writing to tell you that—should you be free to accept—we can offer you an engagement for our next season at the New Theatre, commencing September fourth. The parts for which Sir Laurence has recommended you are 'Portia' in *Julius Caesar*——"

JERRY (*awed*). Blimey!

JACKSON. "—and the 'Player Queen' in *Hamlet*. Our thir production has not yet been decided upon. If you are interested, will you please let me know when it would be convenient for you to come to London and meet our producer, and discuss terms, etc., etc. I am, Yours Faithfully." I can't make out the signature. "Secretary to the Old Vic Company." (*He gives the letter back to* SANDRA.)

(*They immediately all crowd round* SANDRA *congratulating her. Out of the general buzz comes* DAPHNE's *voice.*)

DAPHNE (*rising*). I say. What will *Norwood* say?

NORWOOD (*putting down the cup and newspaper on the table*). He'll say—— (*He speaks in an almost bitter voice.*) Congratulations, my dear Sandra.

(*They all turn.* SANDRA *rises and runs to* NORWOOD.)

SANDRA (*excitedly*). Norwood, you heard?

NORWOOD (*coldly*). Yes, I heard. I stood on the fringe of the crowd, and I heard.

(*There is an uncomfortable silence. The others exchange awkward glances* MAUD *moves to the fireplace and takes her script from the mantelpiece.*

An odd way for a husband to hear of his wife's success.

SANDRA (*hurt*). Norwood.

NORWOOD (*in a vicious undertone*). Don't you think you might have come to me before letting Jackson blurt it out to that mob?

SANDRA (*wretchedly*). Norwood. I'm sorry . . .

NORWOOD. After all, I am your husband.

SANDRA. But don't you see? I was excited. I didn't think . . .

NORWOOD (*bitterly*). Your *husband*. Yes, I suppose *that's* what I shall be in the future, Sandra Layton's husband. (*He turns away from her.*) Oh, God!

SANDRA. Norwood, how can you talk like that? You're not . . . (*Then with horror.*) Oh, God! Norwood—you're not jealous? (*She puts out her hand and touches him.*)

(*He swings away from her.*)

NORWOOD (*savagely*). Oh, leave me alone. (*He strides off up* L.)

SANDRA (*following*). Norwood.

(*They can be seen arguing off up* L. *The* PRODUCER *enters down* L.)

PRODUCER. Come along, come along. Stand by. I feel better now.

(*A* VOICE *is heard calling from the back of the circle.*)

VOICE. Mr Blacker.

PRODUCER (*stopping* C. *and peering out front*). Yes, what is it?

VOICE. There's a man here to see you with a lot of performing cats.

PRODUCER. Performing cats?

VOICE. Yes. He says you advertised for them in *The Stage*.

PRODUCER. What nonsense. I did no such thing. He's come to the wrong theatre. Tell him to take them round to the Hippodrome.

(SANDRA *and* NORWOOD *sit on the sofa off up* L.)

PRODUCER (*turning to* JACKSON). Now, come along. Where had we got to?

JACKSON (*moving to the prompt table; pointedly*). Lady Frazer-Forbes' second line in Act Two. (*He sits at the prompt table.*)

PRODUCER. Ah, yes. Maudie.

(MAUD *moves to the* PRODUCER. AVIS *and* DAPHNE, *not being in this scene in the play, exit up* R.)

Maudie, we'll leave that scene between the two women for the moment. It's got to be cut to ribbons—far too long. (*To* JACKSON.) What happens after that?

(MAUD *moves to the fireplace.*)

JACKSON (*referring to his script*). Lord Fulton-Meyer and his friend, the Honourable Reggie de la Mere, enter.

PRODUCER. My God, we are in the peerage. All right. Stand by, Lord Fulton-Meyer and his friend the Honourable Weston-super-Mare.

(*The* PRODUCER *moves to his corner down* R. SANDRA *rises and enters up* L.)

JACKSON. Jerry, that's you and Norwood. Norwood is playing Lord Thing, isn't he? (*He looks around.*) Oh, where the devil's he got to?

SANDRA. I'll fetch him. (*She moves up* L. *and calls.*) Norwood. Norwood, you're on.

PRODUCER (*moving* C.). I *do* wish people would stand by at rehearsals. It's such a little thing to ask.

(JERRY *moves up* L.C.)

SANDRA (*calling*). *Norwood.*

NORWOOD (*still on the sofa*). All right. All right. Dammit, I heard you. I'm coming. I'm coming. (*He rises.*)

JACKSON (*growling*). Yes, so's Christmas.

PRODUCER. Oh, Jacko, that wasn't worthy of you.

(*The* AUTHOR *enters down* L. *The* PRODUCER *crosses to him and shakes hands warmly.* MAUD *sits in the chair down* R. SANDRA *moves* L. *of the steps.* JERRY *takes an eyeglass from his pocket and puts it in his eye.*)

PRODUCER. Hullo. How are you? Are you all right there, old boy?

(NORWOOD *comes storming through the french window.*)

NORWOOD. Yes, what is it? Where are we? Is it my entrance?

PRODUCER (*coldly*). It is. We've only been waiting five minutes for you, that's all.

NORWOOD (*explosively*). Oh, have you.

PRODUCER (*moving to his corner down* R.; *heavily*). No, no. Please don't apologize. Such a little thing.

JACKSON. Come on, Norwood, enter up left with Jerry.

(NORWOOD *moves up* L. *There is a pause.*)

PRODUCER (*irritably*). Well, come on. Make your entrance.

NORWOOD. Don't we get an entrance cue?

PRODUCER. Oh, for Heaven's sake give them an entrance cue, one of you.

MAUD. Oh, sorry, darling, that's me. (*In part.*) "Shh! That sounds like Geoffrey now."

(NORWOOD *and* JERRY *make an entrance up* L.)

PRODUCER (*interrupting*). Just a minute. Just a minute. That's damn silly. (*To* MAUD.) What's that line again?

MAUD. "Ssh! That sounds like Geoffrey now."

PRODUCER. What does?

MAUD (*vaguely*). What?

PRODUCER. *What* sounds like Geoffrey now? You're not supposed to be psychic, are you? You can't hear sounds other people can't hear. Why should you suddenly out of the blue and for no apparent reason say, "Ssh! That sounds like Geoffrey now"?

MAUD (*testily—for her*). The only reason I said it, darling, was because it's in the script.

PRODUCER. Well, you've got to have a better reason than that. Ah, I know. Norwood, let's hear your voice outside talking to Jerry. Go back on it.

(NORWOOD *and* JERRY "*go off*" *again.*)

PRODUCER. Give Norwood a cue for speaking off, someone.

SANDRA. That's me. (*In part.*) "Don't say any more, Mother, I can't bear it."

PRODUCER. Right. That's you speaking off, Norwood.

NORWOOD (*dully and mechanically*). Buzz, buzz, buzz, buzz.

PRODUCER (*after a slight pause; moving* C.). Don't worry about it now, but if you *could* think of something a little more sparkling. (*He moves down* R.)

NORWOOD (*very surly*). Soda water bottle, soda water bottle, soda water bottle.

PRODUCER (*after a tense pause*). Carry on.

MAUD (*in part; quickly*). "Ssh. That sounds like Geoffrey now."

(NORWOOD *and* JERRY "*enter*". NORWOOD *moves above the table,*
JERRY *to* L. *of the table.*)

"Geoffrey dear. You're very late. Melisande was getting anxious, weren't you, Melisande?"

PRODUCER (*heavily*). "Dear."

MAUD. "Weren't you, *dear*?"

NORWOOD (*in part*). "Oh, I met Reggie and we went along to the club for a drink, didn't we, Reggie?"

PRODUCER (*unconsciously correcting*). "Dear." (*He coughs hastily to cover his mistake.*)

JERRY (*in part, playing it as a Dude of the old-fashioned type*). "Oh, yes, *wather*." (*He gives a very false "silly-ass" laugh.*) "Ha-ha."

(*The* PRODUCER'S *head comes up with a jerk, and the expression on his face is that of a stricken deer. For the moment he says nothing.*)

JERRY (*crossing to* SANDRA *and shaking hands*). "How are you, Lady Fulton-Meyer?" (*He crosses to* MAUD.) "And *dear* Lady Fwazer-Forbes."

(*A tremendous hammering begins off* L. GEORGE *is hard at work on the scenery.* MAUD *attempts to speak through it.*)

MAUD (*her voice getting louder and louder*). "How nice to see you again, Reggie, and how is your mother, *the dear Lady de la Mere?*"
JERRY (*shouting*). Quiet.
JACKSON (*roaring*). *Quiet.*
PRODUCER (*yelling*). QUIET.

(*The knocking continues. The* AUTHOR *moves* C. *and stamps his foot.*)

AUTHOR (*piping*). Quiet.

(*The hammering immediately stops. Everyone gazes at the* AUTHOR *in amazement as he edges* L.)

MAUD (*in part*). "And how is your Mother, the dear Lady de la Mere?"
JERRY (*to the* PRODUCER). Mr Blacker.
PRODUCER (*without looking at him; in a hollow voice*). Yes?
JERRY. Mine is supposed to be a comedy part, isn't it?
PRODUCER (*doubtfully*). Yes.
JERRY. Well, I've thought of a gag that might go in here.
PRODUCER (*without enthusiasm*). Yes?
JERRY (*laughing already at his gag*). Yes. When Maudie says to me, "How is your mother, the dear Lady de la Mere?"—I thought I might say, "The Old Grey *Mare* she ain't what she used to be."

(*He roars with laughter, looking round the company for appreciation. But there is none. The faces of all are frozen. Gradually the laughter freezes in* JERRY *also, and after a glance at the* PRODUCER, *he continues.*)

(*Dejected.*) Oh, all right. (*Resuming his part.*) "The old girl's in gweat form, Lady Fwazer-Forbes. Yes, *wather*—ha-ha." (*Again the laugh.*)

(*The* PRODUCER *is hearing all this through a haze.*)

MAUD (*in part*). "I haven't seen her since the Duchess of Harrogate's soirée in—— (*She pauses and turns a page of her script.*)
PRODUCER. Eighteen forty-nine.
MAUD (*in part*)—in September last."
NORWOOD (*as himself*). Look, Harry, what are we supposed to be doing during all this back chat?
PRODUCER. I don't know. Knitting a jumper, I should think.

(NORWOOD *sits in the chair above the table.*)

JERRY (*stammering*). Oh—oh . . .

PRODUCER (*irritably*). What do you mean, "Oh—oh . . ." Get on with it.

JERRY (*in part*). "Oh, weally? You must call on the old girl one day. She'd be fwightfully bucked. She's going up to Duwham next month for the shooting."

PRODUCER. Why does she have to go up to Duwham for it? Why can't she be shot in London?

AUTHOR (*moving* L.C.). No—no—Mr Blacker. The—shooting—grouse—grouse, you know.

(NORWOOD *rises*.)

PRODUCER (*wearily*). No, I didn't know. Carry on.

(*The* AUTHOR *edges* L.)

NORWOOD (*in part*). "And talking of drinks, I wouldn't say no to a thimble now."

PRODUCER (*completely puzzled and very indignant*). What's he talking to a thimble for? (*He moves* C.) And what's all this about drinks? The last line I heard was that Lady Someone-or-other was going up to Duwham to be shot. What's that got to do with drinks?

(SANDRA *sits in the chair* R. *of the table*.)

NORWOOD. When I first came on I said, "I met Reggie and we went along to the club for a drink."

PRODUCER. When you first came on—yes. But that was hours ago. The audience have had three pages of Debrett recited at them since then. You don't suppose they're going to remember what *you* said after all that, do you?

NORWOOD (*excitedly*). *I* didn't write the damn play.

PRODUCER (*more excited*). I know you didn't. (*He pauses*.) Nobody did! (*He catches the* AUTHOR'S *eye*.) All the same, that line has got to be altered. Make a note of that, will you? Mr Beverley cannot possibly say, "And talking of drinks and thimbles." We must have another line altogether.

AUTHOR (*vaguely*). Oh, another line.

(*He exits down* L.)

PRODUCER (*moving down* R.). Carry on.

SANDRA (*rising; to* NORWOOD). "Little Estelle . . ."

PRODUCER (*aghast*). Little *who*?

SANDRA. Little Estelle.

PRODUCER (*hopelessly*). Oh, all right. Carry on. (*He mutters in his corner about "Little Estelle".*)

SANDRA (*in part*). "Little Estelle was disappointed you were not at home for her birthday party, Geoffrey."

JERRY (*turning to* SANDRA). "I say, Lady Fulton-Meyer, I'm

fwightfully sowwy, J am weally. I'm afwaid it was my fault, yes, by Jove."

PRODUCER. Oh, no, by Jove—that's out.

JERRY (*after a glance at the* PRODUCER). "I say, what a wotter I was to keep you fwom your little daughter's birthday-party. Yes, by Gad, *what a wotter*." (*Again the "silly-ass" laugh.*)

PRODUCER. Do we get much more of that?

JERRY. Much more of what?

PRODUCER. That "what a wotter" gag?

JERRY (*indignant*). Of course. It's my big laugh. It goes right through the play.

PRODUCER (*with feeling*). That's what you think. Carry on.

MAUD (*in part*). "Does Lady de la Mere still attend the Duchess of Pateley's whist drives, Reggie?"

PRODUCER. Oh, God, are we off on that tack again? (*To the audience.*) I've never heard such snobbery in any play. (*He mutters on.*)

JERRY (*in part*). "Wather not, Lady Fwazer-Forbes. The old girl's given the Duchess a wide berth, ever since she caught her playing with six aces in the pack."

MAUD (*in part*). "Oh."

JERRY (*in part*). "Yes wather. Our family dwaws the line at five."

MAUD. That's you, Jacko.

(JACKSON *rises and crosses down* R.)

PRODUCER (*irritably*). Oh, come on, Jacko, do stand by.

JACKSON. Well, I can't be everywhere, can I? (*Then, in part.*) "Dinner is served."

PRODUCER. Yes, and they're open. Let's have a drink. All right, everyone, break for ten minutes.

(MAUD *and* JERRY *exit up* R.)

NORWOOD. Well, I'm going over to the *George and Dragon*. (*He moves* L.) If I'm wanted, send someone to *carry* me out.

(*He exits* L. SANDRA *follows him, expostulating.*)

JACKSON (*calling*). George, save those lights.

(*He exits* R.)

GEORGE (*off; calling*). Aye, aye.

(*The* VOICE *is heard calling again from the back of the circle.*)

VOICE. Mr Blacker.

PRODUCER (*peering out front*). Yes, what is it?

VOICE. That man with the cats is still here.

PRODUCER (*annoyed*). I cannot see the man with the cats. Tell him to go away.

Voice. He says he won't go until you've paid the cats' fares back to London.

Producer (*moving to the bridge*). Oh, Lord! All right. Tell him I'm coming.

As he steps on to the bridge to cross into the auditorium, the stage lights go out. He gives a yell of terror, there is a terrific and prolonged crash as he falls into the orchestra pit, then silence. After a few moments the house-lights go on and the Producer *is no longer to be seen. The* Curtain *remains up.*

ACT III

SCENE.—*The same. Twenty minutes later.*

The LIGHTS *on the stage come on. The house-lights fade.* GEORGE, *very subdued, enters slowly up* R., *moves down* C. *and stares into the orchestra pit in much the same way that he would stare into a grave. He removes his cap.* MARY, *crying, enters down* L., *moves* L. *of* GEORGE *and stands beside him also looking into the orchestra pit. After a few moments they turn and look at each other and* MARY *bursts into a noisy "Boo-hoo".* GEORGE *looks as if he might do the same.*

MARY (*through her tears*). Oh, George.
GEORGE (*in a quavering voice*). I didn't do it on purpose, I swear I didn't. I'd 'ave cut off me right 'and rather than 'ave it 'appen.

(MAUD, *dabbing her eyes with her handkerchief, enters down* R. *She puts her script on the mantelpiece, moves* R. *of* GEORGE, *looks sadly into the orchestra pit, then looks at him more in sorrow than in anger.*)

(*Unhappily.*) Miss Barron—I . . .
MAUD (*choking*). Oh, George.
GEORGE. Miss Barron, you don't think that I . . .
MAUD. Oh, George. (*She bursts into tears again.*)
GEORGE (*miserably*). Oh, 'ell.

(*He turns and exits mournfully* L. MARY, *still weeping, moves to the form below the table and sits.* MAUD *turns and moves* R. *of* MARY.)

MAUD. We must all be very brave, darling. (*Then, a little annoyed.*) I *know* that's a line from a play, but I did mean it, dear.
MARY. H-h-how is he? Have you heard?

(MAUD *shakes her head and draws in a long breath. One rather gathers that the cortège should just about have reached the cemetery gates.* MARY *weeps, and weeps.*)

MAUD. The doctor is still with him, dear. We can but hope
MARY. You don't think George really put the lights out on purpose, do you?
MAUD. I don't blame George, dear. I hold Jacko responsible for what's happened.
MARY. But, Maudie, Mr Harley wasn't anywhere near the stage when it happened. He was over in the pub standing everyone drinks and I was in the storeroom under the stage.
MAUD. I'm not saying that Jacko *did* it, Mary; merely that he was responsible for it happening. He tempted Providence—or

whatever it is you do tempt. He said it was a pity Harry hadn't
fallen off the bridge the first time George put the lights out, and
he also told George—of course, I *know* he was only joking, dear—
he told George that if he saw Harry come anywhere near the
stage he was to drop a counter-weight on his head. And if that
isn't tempting Providence—or whatever it is you do tempt—I'd
like to know what is.

MARY. It was a terrible shock when I found him unconscious.

MAUD (*moving down* C. *and looking into the orchestra pit*). How he
managed to crawl out of the orchestra well and under the stage
I don't know. (*She moves* R. *of* MARY.) Mary, I shall never forget
seeing them carry him upstairs, never. I was in the corridor outside my dressing-room and I thought they were bringing the
settee they'd been promising me for months, but when I saw it
was poor bruised, bleeding Harry—oh, my dear.

(JERRY *enters up* R. *and moves to* L. *of the steps.*)

Have you heard any more news, Jerry?

JERRY (*soberly*). Jacko spoke to me for a second, just now. The
doctor says it may be very serious.

MAUD (*in horror*). Jerry, you don't mean that he might—might
—oh, I can't say it.

JERRY (*shrugging his shoulders*). They don't know yet, but the
doctor says that even if he doesn't—doesn't—you know—his
brain will be affected for the rest of his life.

MARY (*perfectly sincerely*). Oh dear, and it was a bit affected
already, wasn't it?

MAUD (*suddenly*). I know what it is. It's those nuns. Everything
has gone wrong since they came. First that author creature had
to turn up. Then Sandra got the Old Vic offer. Then Avis had a
letter from her father saying she'd got to give up the stage. And
Harry. Have you ever known Harry more bad-tempered or im-
possible than—not that I wanted to speak ill of the dead. (*Then
with horror.*) Oh dear, what am I saying? Of course, he isn't yet,
is he? Oh, now I'm making it worse, but you see what I mean,
don't you?

(*The* AUTHOR *enters down* L. *He is very dishevelled and hot from running. He carries several packets of cotton wool, bandages, an air
cushion, some bottles and has a harrassed expression. The others look
at him with neither rapture nor joy.* JERRY *moves up* R.C. *in exaspera-
tion.*)

AUTHOR. Will it be all right if I take these up to Mr Blacker's
room?

JERRY (*curtly*). You'd better take 'em right away.

AUTHOR (*dithering*). Oh, yes. I'm—er—I'm afraid I don't know
where it is.

MAUD. It's up the stairs.

AUTHOR. Oh, yes, of course. (*He hurries up* R., *running up the short flight of steps and over the back of them. He drops half his packages, and a loose bandage unrolls behind him.*)

MAUD. I'll show you the way.

(*She moves* R. MARY *rises and follows, picking up the packages and the loose end of the bandage as she goes. The* AUTHOR, MAUD *and* MARY *exit up* R. AVIS, *weeping to herself, enters down* R.)

JERRY. Oh, God, don't *you* start crying.

AVIS (*sniffing*). I'm not.

JERRY. You jolly well are. (*He comes to her and with no show of tenderness takes her face in his two hands, burlesquing.*) I can see the tears welling up in those dark liquid pools.

(AVIS *just stands looking at him. He continues to hold her face in his hands. It is as if he is really seeing her for the first time, and liking what he sees.*)

I'm sorry, duckie. My "light comedy" is a bit on the heavy side, isn't it? (*He pauses.*) You're leaving the company soon, aren't you?

AVIS (*nodding*). M'mm.

JERRY. Little country mouse going home, eh?

AVIS. Yes—little country mouse going home. (*She weeps.*)

JERRY (*furious with himself*). Oh, God, I've done it again. I ought to be kicked in the pants. (*His arms go round her, comforting her.*) Don't cry, Avis. You're not a little mouse—that is—(*he takes her face in his hands again*)—if you are, you're a very attractive one. Has anyone ever told you that?

(AVIS *shakes her head.* JERRY *suddenly takes her in his arms and kisses her. It is a long kiss. When they finally come out of it,* JERRY *stares at her in amazement.*)

JERRY. How long have you been with us now?

AVIS. Three months.

JERRY. I must be losing my grip. But you—(*anxiously*)—you're not leaving for a fortnight yet, are you?

AVIS. No, Jerry.

JERRY (*babbling somewhat*). And you'll—you'll give me your address before you go? I—I—I mean—Harry's promised me a week off soon—so—I could come down and see you—that is—if . . . (*He kisses her.*)

(MAUD *enters down* R.)

MAUD (*murmuring*). Where did I leave my knitting. (*She crosses to* L.C. *below* AVIS *and* JERRY, *then stops suddenly and "double takes" them.*)

(SANDRA *enters hurriedly down* L.)

SANDRA. Has anyone been wanting me or Norwood?

(AVIS *and* JERRY *break.* AVIS *moves above the steps.*)

JERRY. Wanting you? Good Lord, don't you know what's happened?

SANDRA. Happened? What do you mean?

JERRY. You don't know about Harry?

(MAUD *searches for her knitting up* C. JERRY *moves to* AVIS *and gazes fondly at her.*)

SANDRA. What about Harry?

MAUD. My dear, *terrible.* He fell into the orchestra well. Mary found him unconscious under the stage. The doctor's with him now. Of course, he *may* live . . .

SANDRA. But—what's happening about rehearsal—and everything?

MAUD. We don't know, dear. We're just waiting till Jacko comes and tells us something.(*She turns to* JERRY.) Jerry.

JERRY (*gazing at* AVIS). Yes?

MAUD. I think I must have left my knitting in my dressing-room. Jerry, would you go to see?

JERRY (*vacantly*). What do you want me to go to sea for?

MAUD. Would you go to see if my knitting's up in my room?

JERRY (*realizing*). What? Oh, yes, rather. (*To* AVIS. *Fondly.*) Coming?

AVIS. Oh, yes.

(JERRY *and* AVIS *exit hand in hand up* R. SANDRA *moves to the prompt table, and sits on it.*)

MAUD (*after watching* SANDRA *a few moments*). I suppose it's wicked to talk of anything else but poor Harry, but—(*she crosses and puts an arm round* SANDRA)—but, Sandra, I *am* so pleased for you—about the Old Vic offer, I mean.

(SANDRA *is silent.*)

You deserve it, my dear, and ever since I've known you I've felt that one day something like this would happen. How does it go? "There is a tide in the affairs of men which . . ."

SANDRA (*beginning almost inaudibly*). ". . . which, taken at the flood, leads on to fortune; omitted—(*she pauses, then slowly*)—all the voyage of their life is bound in shallows—and in miseries. On such a full sea are we now afloat; and we must take the current when it serves, or—lose our ventures." (*She pauses, then with a sad little laugh.*) *Julius Caesar.*

MAUD. But, Sandra, you have no *doubts* about what you're going to do—have you?

SANDRA (*rising*). It isn't as easy as all that, darling. At first— when the letter came—I had no doubts. I don't think I had any feelings beyond sheer amazement that anything like that could have happened to me. But since then I've had time to think—and I'll have to think an awful lot more—about——

E

MAUD (*after a slight pause*). Norwood?

SANDRA.—Norwood. (*She crosses below the steps.*)

MAUD (*moving to* SANDRA). I know, darling, you won't like being parted from him; that's always—unpleasant. I know that sometimes John and I felt that we . . .

SANDRA. But with Norwood and me, it isn't quite the same thing. (*She pauses.*) You see, Maudie, I know that if we part now, it won't just be for a while—it will be for good. (*She sits on the steps.*)

MAUD (*quietly*). Sandra. Norwood hasn't said that.

SANDRA. No. He hasn't. But within two minutes of telling him about the letter, I knew it to be so. (*She pauses. Simply.*) I love Norwood. I know that he's weak; I know that as far as making a name for himself—he's had it. He's a good actor; sometimes a brilliant one, but he just hasn't the necessary guts to fight his way to the top. He has to feel on top all the time. *Here*, he is on top. The audience love him. You know that, Maudie, he just can't go wrong, in their eyes. And—that's the way he likes it. That's Norwood—a big fish—in a little pond.

MAUD. But surely he can go on being a big fish . . .

SANDRA. No—he couldn't. How is a man with a mind like that going to react to the fact that his wife is playing in London with the finest company in the country, while he—Maudie, it wouldn't work. He's been drinking a lot lately. If I accept this offer, God knows what will happen to him. I love Norwood, with all his faults. I love him, but I love my job, too. And if I can make a success of it it means money in the future—and surely that means everything. Isn't there some way I can compromise, or does it mean just the choice of "husband" or "career"?

MAUD. Surely he *must* see it from your point of view. He isn't supporting you. You're working, just the same as he is. You're both putting money into the family kitty. So how can he grumble because you happen to get the better job?

SANDRA. I see that, dear, but—Norwood won't.

(NORWOOD *enters up* R. *and moves to* L. *of the steps.* MAUD *breaks to* R. *of the table.*)

NORWOOD. I thought we were supposed to be rehearsing a play.

SANDRA (*rising*). Darling, something terrible has happened. Poor Harry . . .

(MAUD *sits in the chair* R. *of the table.*)

NORWOOD. To hell with Harry. The man's a fool. Doesn't know the first thing about production . . .

SANDRA (*sharply*). Norwood, don't talk like that. For all we know he may be dead, or dying, at this very moment.

NORWOOD (*somewhat shaken, fumbling for a cigarette*). What? What are you talking about? Have you got a cigarette?

(SANDRA *and* NORWOOD *move to the form up* C. *and sit.* SANDRA *takes a packet of cigarettes from her handbag and offers it to* NORWOOD. *The* AUTHOR, *still carrying his medical supplies, enters up* R. *He walks absent-mindedly over the back of the steps and down them, then moves to* MAUD *and offers her one of the bottles.*)

AUTHOR. I suppose you wouldn't care for a bottle of iodine— or any of these?

MAUD (*frigidly*). No—thank you.

AUTHOR (*crossing below the table to* L.). They didn't want them when I took them upstairs. The doctor had brought his own. I wish someone would tell me where to put them.

MAUD. Couldn't you just take them home?

AUTHOR. What, all the way to Exeter?

(*The* AUTHOR *exits* L. JERRY, *singing gaily, enters down* R.)

MAUD (*reprovingly*). Jerry.

(JERRY, *abashed, stops singing and sits on the steps.* MARY *enters up* R. *and moves* C.)

MARY. Mr Harley's coming down to speak to the company in a minute. He wants everybody on the stage. Do you think it would be all right if I sounded the gong? I mean, Mr Blacker won't hear it. He's unconscious.

(*She bursts into tears, exits* L. *and re-enters immediately with the gong and stick.*)

MAUD. Has the doctor gone yet, Mary?

MARY. He'll be leaving any minute.

(JACKSON *and a* DOCTOR *enter up* R. *and stand conversing in an undertone.*)

Here he is. (*She begins to bang the gong funereally, one heavy stroke every two or three seconds.*)

(AVIS *enters down* R., *and sits in the chair down* R. DAPHNE *enters* L. *and moves above the table.*)

DAPHNE (*as she enters*). Is he . . . ? (*The noise of the gong stops her.*)

MAUD (*rising suddenly*). I can't stand that any longer. (*She moves to* MARY, *takes the gong and stick from her and throws them off* L.) He isn't dead yet. (*She moves to the chair* R. *of the table and sits.*)

(*The* AUTHOR *enters* L. *hopping on one leg, leaving no doubt as to where the gong landed.* JACKSON *and the* DOCTOR *cross slowly to* L. *The* AUTHOR *exits down* L. MARY *sits on the floor below the prompt table.*)

JACKSON (*to the* DOCTOR *as they cross*). Well, thank you very much indeed, Doctor. I'll get on the phone right away about that. And shall I give you a ring after you've examined him at the hospital, or will you ring me?

(JACKSON *and the* DOCTOR *exit* L. *There is silence for a few moments, then the* AUTHOR *enters down* L. *He is cowed by the silence and sits hastily in the* PRODUCER's *chair.*)

MAUD (*rising quickly; with a wail*). No. Not there. (*She moves down* L.C.) Not in his chair.

AUTHOR (*rising hurriedly*). No, no, of course not, I'm sorry. (*He moves and stands* R. *of the door.*)

MAUD (*murmuring*). No-one sits there. (*She unconsciously sits in the* PRODUCER's *chair herself.*)

(*The whole company give a startled yell.* MAUD *rises quickly, moves to the chair* L. *of the table and sits.* JACKSON *enters down* L. *He is subdued, but under it all he is aware that he is now in charge. He takes in the company with a glance, then moves slowly and deliberately to the position down* R. *from which the* PRODUCER *usually works. There is a pause, then he addresses the company.*)

JACKSON. Ladies and gentlemen. You are, of course, all aware of the—er—tragedy that has overtaken our little fellowship of players.

(GEORGE *enters up* L. *and stands listening.*)

Our producer—our—er—*friend*, Mr Harry Blacker, has met with an accident, the seriousness of which is not yet fully known. The doctor, whom you saw with me just now, insists upon a thorough examination at the hospital. In the meanwhile, he has done what he can for our—er—*dear* friend.

(GEORGE *blows his nose with gusto.*)

(*He glares at* GEORGE.) Our dear friend who, at this moment is lying unconscious in his room upstairs. Without wishing to twist the knife in the wound which I am sure is already in your hearts, I should like to tell you of one little incident which occurred as I stood over the tortured body of our *beloved* friend a short while ago. For one moment he regained consciousness—his eyes met mine—and as I took his outstretched hand he murmured: "Jacko, The Play's the Thing." Just that. Nothing more. But those few words, written by the greatest dramatist of all time—and spoken to me by—and I say it in all sincerity—by the finest producer of all times. . . .

MARY (*tearfully*). Hear, hear.

JACKSON. Shh! Those few words convinced me that I—that all of us—have a duty to perform; a duty to our public, to the "Drama"—but, above all, a duty to that bruised and battered body upstairs.

(DAPHNE *collapses into the chair above the table with a subdued wail.*)

Like Pagliacci—and are we not all Pagliaccis—we must hide our grief and strive, in our own unskilled way to make this play at least a *shadow* of the thing of beauty——

(*The* AUTHOR *applauds feebly.*)

—a shadow of the thing of beauty we know it would have become in his unerring hands.

(*He waits for a round of applause. It doesn't come He turns disgustedly and leans against the proscenium* R. *The* AUTHOR *then decides that he must say a few words. As he begins to speak he notices the end of a roll of bandage hanging out of his pocket. He pulls at it and as it unrolls tries to dispose of it up his sleeve, etc. At the sound of his voice the cast look round amazed.*)

AUTHOR. Ladies and gentlemen—may I, as the—er—stranger within your gates, the—er—visitor in your midst, the—er——

JERRY (*quietly*). The nigger in the wood pile.

AUTHOR.—the nigger in the —ahem—may I commiserate with you in your great sorrow. My association with Mr Blacker has been of all too short a duration. . . .

(JACKSON *suddenly strides* C. GEORGE *exits down* L. *The* AUTHOR, *unheard, continues his speech.*)

JACKSON. Oh, Lord!

MAUD. What's the matter?

JACKSON. The ambulance.

SANDRA. The what?

JACKSON. The ambulance. I've forgotten to order it. The doctor told me to get it right away. (*He sees the* AUTHOR *and crosses to him.*) Look, old boy, you're doing nothing at the moment, are you? Would you mind?

AUTHOR. Mind?

JACKSON. Be a good fellow and get hold of an ambulance from somewhere will you?

AUTHOR. An ambulance?

JACKSON. Yes. I don't know how you do it quite. Ring up an emergency number, don't you? "Something, something, one—two, one—two."

MAUD. No, dear, that's the B.B.C.

JACKSON. Well, anyway, they'll tell you at the box office. Just find out *where* you phone, and then phone. O.K.?

AUTHOR (*flustered*). Oh, yes, yes, of course, certainly. Now—er how do I get to the box office. Oh, yes, of course, through the auditorium.

(*He crosses to the bridge and is about to step on it when there is a yell from the whole company.* MAUD *leaps to her feet.*)

ALL (*ad. lib.*). No. No. No. Not that way. Too risky. Don't do it.

(MAUD *runs to the* AUTHOR *and grabs his right arm,* JACKSON *grabs the* AUTHOR'S *left arm and they back him away from the bridge.*)

JACKSON (*looking at the bridge, then at the* AUTHOR). No.

(*The* AUTHOR *backs away from the bridge, terrified.*)

AUTHOR. No, no, of course not. I'll go round by the stage door.

(*The* AUTHOR *exits hurriedly down* L.)

MAUD (*moving to the fireplace for her script*). I shan't know a moment's peace until that man is out of the theatre for ever. (*She takes her script from the mantelpiece.*)

JACKSON (*busily moving to the prompt table*). Now, come along, everyone, we must get on. Remember his words, "The Play's the Thing".

DAPHNE. This one isn't.

JACKSON (*looking through his script*). Now, where had we got to?

JERRY. We hadn't really got anywhere. I should just stick a pin in one of the pages and start from there.

JACKSON. No. No. I've got it.

(*As he speaks the others take up their positions.* AVIS *rises, crosses and sits up* L. MAUD *sits in the chair down* R. JERRY *rises and stands* L. *of* MAUD. DAPHNE *rises, moves and sits up* L. *with* AVIS. SANDRA *moves* R. *of the table,* NORWOOD *sits in the chair* L. *of the table.* MARY *remains seated on the floor down* L.)

Act Two, where I come on and announce, "Dinner is served." (*He moves down* R.) Let's go from there. Jerry, Norwood, Sandra and you, Maudie, you're on. Clear stage, rest of you. Ready? (*In part.*) "Dinner is served." (*He crosses to the prompt table and sits.*)

MAUD (*rising; reading her script*). "Will you give me your arm, Reggie? Melisande—Geoffrey . . ." (*She is absorbed in her script which she is holding in her right hand.*)

'JERRY *also looking at his script which he is holding in his right hand, holds out his left arm.* MAUD *puts her left arm through his from the front and during the remainder of her speech they circle round and round each other, their interlocked arms acting as a pivot.*)

"I remember the first time I ever saw you, Reggie. You were only a baby, of course. It was at the Marchioness of Buntingford's conversatzione. . . ." (*She realizes they are circling.*) What on earth are you doing, Jerry?

(*She withdraws her arm and followed by* JERRY, *exits down* R. *They re-enter a few moments later up* R. *and sit on the form up* C.)

SANDRA (*to* NORWOOD). You move down to the door, darling.

NORWOOD (*sulkily*). What?

SANDRA. You move down to the door and I call you back.

NORWOOD (*rising*). We'll take the move for granted now. Carry on with your lines.

SANDRA (*after an anxious look at him*). "Geoffrey, I want you to divorce me."

NORWOOD (*reading*). "What? What are you talking about?"

JACKSON (*trying to attract* SANDRA's *attention*). Sandra.

NORWOOD (*looking irritably at* JACKSON, *but continuing with his lines*). "You must be mad. On what grounds?"

JACKSON (*still trying to attract* SANDRA's *attention*). Sandra.

NORWOOD (*loudly and irritably looking at* JACKSON). "And for what reason?" (*He breaks off.*) What the devil's the matter, old boy?

JACKSON (*rather testily*). I just wanted to tell Sandra that she moves down right on the line, "I want you to divorce me." We've got to get these moves right. Go back on it, Sandra.

NORWOOD (*losing his patience*). *Must* we go back on it? Surely to God she can remember a little move like that?

SANDRA. Norwood.

(*Everyone on the stage is watching them.*)

NORWOOD. All right, all right, go back on it. Waste the whole day on it. I don't mind.

SANDRA (*moving down* R.; *reading*). "I want you to divorce me."

NORWOOD (*reading, with bad grace, and following her*). "What? What are you talking about? On what grounds and for what reason?"

SANDRA. "I will provide the grounds, and the reason is surely obvious enough . . ."

NORWOOD. "You mean . . ."

SANDRA. "Geoffrey—I want a little happiness out of life. That isn't such a great deal to ask. But I know that as long as I remain your wife . . ." (*She turns and faces* NORWOOD.)

(NORWOOD *is looking at* SANDRA, *not at his script.*)

(*She gives him his cue again.*) "As long as I remain your wife . . . (*As herself, a suspicion of a break in her voice.*) It's a broken sentence, darling.

(*There is a short pause.*)

NORWOOD (*quietly*). Sorry. (*He reads.*) "Have I failed so miserably in my duties as a husband, then?"

SANDRA (*reading; flatly*). "Your drinking I can forgive—since it would appear to be so indispensable to you. But your undisguised contempt of me; your blatant ridiculing of me in front of others—no, Geoffrey, that I cannot, and will not, tolerate." (*As herself, to* JACKSON.) I *do* sit here, don't I?

(JACKSON *is watching the scene intently, but more from the* SANDRA-NORWOOD *angle than the characters in the play. He starts and refers to the script.*)

JACKSON. What? Yes, that's right, darling, sit easy chair.

(SANDRA *sits in the chair down* R.)

NORWOOD (*reading*). "You will have difficulty in persuading a judge to give you a divorce on those grounds, I fancy."

SANDRA (*reading*). "I've told you before—I will give you sufficient grounds."

NORWOOD (*reading*). "Ah! Now we're getting nearer the truth. And why don't you admit it, my dear Melisande?" (*He uses his* "*My dear Sandra*" *inflection.*)

MAUD (*rising quickly*). "Why don't you admit it, my dear Melisande?" That's me. (*She crosses down* R. *and makes an entrance as from the dining-room.*) "Melisande, Geoffrey, why on earth don't you come in to dinner?"

SANDRA (*reading*). "I'm sorry, Mother, but there is something I had to discuss with Geoffrey."

MAUD. "But, Melisande. . . ."

SANDRA. "Leave us, Mother, please."

NORWOOD. "On the contrary, I think your mother should stay."

MAUD. "There's nothing wrong, is there?"

DAPHNE (*rising*). Oh, I'm off. I mean, I'm on. (*She makes an entrance* L.)

MAUD (*crossing to* DAPHNE). "Rose."

DAPHNE (*referring to her script*). "Yes, madam."

MAUD (*referring to her script*). "Leave the room."

DAPHNE. "Yes, madam." (*To* JACKO *as she returns to her chair up* L.) Hell of a fine entrance that is. (*She sits.*)

MAUD (*turning to* NORWOOD *and* SANDRA). "Melisande, won't you tell me what is wrong?"

SANDRA. "Not now, Mother. Leave us, please. Make our excuses to Reggie. We'll be with you shortly."

MAUD. "But, Melisande . . ."

SANDRA. "Mother—please!"

MAUD. "Oh, very well, dear." (*She crosses down* R.) Bit of a drip, this woman, isn't she?

(*She exits down* R.)

SANDRA (*rising*). "Nothing matters but the definite fact that I must get away from you, Geoffrey."

JACKSON. Cross to the fireplace, dear.

SANDRA (*easing down* R.). "Somewhere where I can forget the past few years of misery I have endured as your wife, and forget also—I pray God—the happy memory of us as we once were."

(*There is a pause.*)

JACKSON. Carry on.

NORWOOD. "Haven't I given you everything it was in my power to give?"

(MAUD *enters up* R. *and sits on the form with* JERRY, *up* C.)

SANDRA. "Materially, yes. But, Geoffrey, there are so many things in life so much more precious than the things you've given me."

NORWOOD (*reading*). "Pah! You talk like a romantic school-girl." (*As himself.*) And, by God, she does and all. This scene's got to be cut, Jacko. I'm not going to learn all this slush.

JACKSON (*firmly*). Now, carry on, Norwood, carry on.

(NORWOOD *looks for a moment as if he is going to argue with* JACKSON. *Then with compressed lips he returns to his part. He is now definitely sulk-ing and his lines are spoken without expression and almost inaudibly.*)

NORWOOD. "You talk like a romantic schoolgirl. You've made your bed, my dear Melisande, and you must lie on it. And a very comfortable bed it is, if you will allow me to say so. If I had be-trayed you by thought, word or deed, then I would have done as you desire, but with my hand on my heart I say to you . . ."

(*Suddenly the* PRODUCER's *voice rings out hollowly from the back of the theatre, high up in the auditorium. He has a bandage round his head and his right arm in a sling.*)

PRODUCER. "Oh, pardon me, thou bleeding piece of earth, that I am meek and gentle with these *butchers*."

(*There is a horrified silence; everyone on the stage stares towards the audience.*)

(*He calls again.*) Can you hear me down there? I say, can you hear me down there, because I'm damned if I can hear you up here!

(*The tension is broken. Exclamations break out from the company.* JERRY, AVIS, DAPHNE *and* MAUD *rise.* MAUD *moves down* C.)

MAUD (*after a pause, in a hushed voice*). He's dead. It's his ghost.

(*The company peer out front trying to find the* PRODUCER.)

JACKSON. Dead? No such luck. That's him all right. (*He shouts.*) Where are you, Harry?

PRODUCER. Back of the circle. (*Or "Up in the gallery."*)

MAUD (*shouting*). But you shouldn't be. You should be in your room unconscious.

JACKSON (*shouting*). Do you realize we'd almost given you up for dead?

PRODUCER. If I have to listen to Norwood mumbling through his part for another five minutes, you can.

(MAUD *sits in the chair* L. *of the table.*)

Norwood. How long have you been in this profession?

(NORWOOD *starts to tell him, but the* PRODUCER *interrupts.* DAPHNE *sits in the chair above the table.*)

All right, all right, don't tell if you don't want to. But from your performance during the last five minutes one would imagine you'd done nothing else but walking on parts for the local Co-operative Dramatic Society.

(NORWOOD *turns angrily and sits on the steps.* SANDRA *moves to the steps and sits on them below* NORWOOD.)

JACKSON. Oh, Lord, he's off.

PRODUCER (*sharply*). What's that, Jacko? What did you say? I couldn't hear a word.

JACKSON (*yelling*). You weren't meant to.

PRODUCER. All this mumbling, mumbling, mumbling. First Norwood and now you. What's the matter with you all? Can't you speak out—bring your voices forward. Good God, have I got to come down there and give you all elocution lessons. As my old chief used to say——

(*There are groans and protests from all on the stage.*)

—the man who's stood in a queue for an hour and paid his shilling for a hard seat in the gallery has as much right to know what the play's about as the man who's booked a comfortable stall and drifts in half-way through the first act.

JERRY (*to the others*). He'll have us all singing *The Red Flag* in a minute.

PRODUCER (*yelling*). Who said that? Who said that about *The Red Flag*?

JERRY (*embarrassed*). I did.

PRODUCER (*furious*). Oh, you did, did you? One more crack like that out of you and you'll be out of this theatre on your backside. *Maudie.*

MAUD (*rising, thoroughly cowed, and moving down* L.). Yes?

PRODUCER. That entrance of yours just now—dreadful. This woman you're playing—Lady Somebody-or-other. . . .

MAUD. Lady Frazer-Forbes.

PRODUCER (*derisively*). Lady Frazer-Forbes. A dignified dowager, probably belonging to one of the best families in England, and you waddle on to the stage like a peevish penguin.

(MAUD *breaks up* C. *The* AUTHOR *enters up* R. *and trots across to* JACKSON.)

AUTHOR (*excitedly*). I've done it, Mr Harley. I've ordered the ambulance.

PRODUCER (*livid*). Clear that man off the stage. Who is he? *Who is he?* How many times have I said I will not have artistes bringing their friends back stage to rehearsal.

JACKSON (*to the* AUTHOR; *pathetically*). Go away, for God's sake.

(*The* AUTHOR *is completely bewildered by the situation. He has not yet realized that it is the* PRODUCER *who is raving out front.*)

Aᴜᴛʜᴏʀ (*looking out front and at* Jᴀᴄᴋsᴏɴ *alternately*). But—
but . . .

Pʀᴏᴅᴜᴄᴇʀ. Am I the producer in this theatre or am I not?

Aᴜᴛʜᴏʀ (*not believing*). Mr Harley. That surely isn't Mr Blacker
out there, is it?

(Jᴀᴄᴋsᴏɴ *puts his head in his hands and sways to and fro in his misery*.)

Jᴀᴄᴋsᴏɴ (*almost in tears*). Go away. Go away.

Pʀᴏᴅᴜᴄᴇʀ (*almost demented*). If that man isn't outside this theatre
in two minutes, I'll come down and throw him out myself.

(*The* Aᴜᴛʜᴏʀ *jumps about down* ᴄ. *in complete bewilderment*.)

Aᴜᴛʜᴏʀ (*in a little piping voice*). But—but—Mr Blacker. Don't
you see who it is? It's me—*me*. (*He strikes his bosom with both hands.
Pathetically*.) I'm so glad you're better.

Pʀᴏᴅᴜᴄᴇʀ. Will someone be kind enough to tell me what this
half-wit is blithering about?

Jᴀᴄᴋsᴏɴ (*raising his head slightly*). I—I . . . (*He shakes his head
wearily and buries it in his hands again*.)

Mᴀᴜᴅ (*moving down to* ʟ. *of the* Aᴜᴛʜᴏʀ *and shouting to the* Pʀᴏᴅᴜᴄᴇʀ). It's the author, dear.

Pʀᴏᴅᴜᴄᴇʀ. The what?

Mᴀᴜᴅ (*prodding the* Aᴜᴛʜᴏʀ *with her finger*). He's trying to tell
you he's the author. (*To the* Aᴜᴛʜᴏʀ.) Aren't you?

(*The* Aᴜᴛʜᴏʀ *looks out front and wags his head up and down very
vigorously in assent*.)

(*To the* Pʀᴏᴅᴜᴄᴇʀ.) He's been to get an ambulance for you. (*To
the* Aᴜᴛʜᴏʀ.) Haven't you?

(*The* Aᴜᴛʜᴏʀ's *head wags vigorously again*.)

Pʀᴏᴅᴜᴄᴇʀ (*alarmed*). Good God! They don't bring an ambulance
on in this play, do they?

Mᴀᴜᴅ (*now completely finished*). It isn't true. It isn't true. It can't
be happening.

Pʀᴏᴅᴜᴄᴇʀ (*loudly and warningly*). What's that, Maudie? I can't
hear you. You're mumbling.

(Mᴀᴜᴅ *lets out a piercing scream, throws up her hands, moves to the chair
ʀ. of the table and sits*.)

Now, now. None of that. You know my rule. No temperaments in
this theatre. Now come along, everybody. Let's see if we can't get
something into this scene. Jacko. Go back a bit. Start them off
from Maudie's entrance from the dining-room. Stand by, everybody, I'll be down there with you in a minute.

(Jᴇʀʀʏ *and* Aᴠɪs *sit on the form up* ᴄ.)

Jᴀᴄᴋsᴏɴ (*yelling*). Clear the stage.

(*The* AUTHOR *moves wretchedly to* R. *of the door.* NORWOOD *rises and throws his script down on the stage.*)

NORWOOD (*loudly*). I'm getting out of this. Tell that screaming half-wit when he comes down, that I'm through. (*He moves down* R.)

SANDRA (*rising from the steps and moving to* NORWOOD). Norwood. Don't be a fool. You can't just walk out like this.

NORWOOD (*turning on* SANDRA). And who are you to tell me what I can and can't do. What's it matter to you? You're sitting pretty, anyway. A nice fat London contract in your pocket. You can afford to laugh at Blacker and his cheap sarcasms.

SANDRA. Norwood . . .

NORWOOD. Don't you worry about me, my dear Sandra. You look after Number One. You're going places. (*With a derisive laugh.*) And so am I. Blackpool.

SANDRA (*in a quiet voice*). Why go to Blackpool and leave me here?

(*Everyone is watching this scene.*)

NORWOOD (*startled; quietly*). What?

SANDRA. Rather ridiculous keeping two homes going, isn't it? Two can live as cheaply as one.

NORWOOD. But this Old Vic offer. Do you mean to say you're not going to accept it?

SANDRA. No—I'm not.

(*There is general consternation.*)

NORWOOD. Sandra . . .

SANDRA. Do you think I want to go mad?

NORWOOD. What do you mean?

SANDRA (*making it convincing to* NORWOOD). "Portia" in *Julius Caesar*—two short scenes; the "Player Queen" in *Hamlet*—one very short scene; and the third play, possibly something smaller or even a walk on. I couldn't stand it; I know I'd rather have the work of learning a fresh and exciting part every week than going on month after month in two small and rather dull ones. (*She pauses. Then perhaps a little too brightly.*) So—there we are.

(NORWOOD *is rather shaken. He takes* SANDRA *by the arm and leads her to the steps, speaking in a gentler voice than he has ever used to her.*)

NORWOOD (*sincerely*). Listen, darling.

(SANDRA *reacts to the very sincere* "*darling*".)

We'll talk about it after rehearsal. Shall we? Come and sit down.

(NORWOOD *and* SANDRA *sit on the steps.* JACKSON, *seated at the prompt table, puts his head in his hands. The* AUTHOR *exits* L. *There is a pause, then the* PRODUCER *appears in one of the boxes.*)

PRODUCER (*coldly and sarcastically*). I see. A Quaker's meeting.

(AVIS, DAPHNE and JERRY *rise hurriedly*.)

PRODUCER (*with cruel politeness*). No, no. *Please.* Don't let me disturb your devotions. I see Jacko hasn't quite finished yet.

JACKSON (*rising quickly and moving behind the* PRODUCER'S *chair*). One of these days, Harry, I'm going to get my hands round that neck of yours, and I'm going to squeeze, and squeeze and squeeze. (*He squeezes an imaginary neck in the* PRODUCER'S *chair*.)

PRODUCER (*calmly*). What a good actor you are, Jacko—when you're not acting.

JACKSON (*rushing to the onstage end of the bridge; wildly*). Let me get at him. Let me get at him.

PRODUCER (*his voice like thunder*). Jacko.

(*Everything stops.*)

(*In a quiet, dignified and hurt voice.*) May I ask you to remember where you are? You're in a theatre, a theatre—the temple of Thespis. The founder of—*the drama.* Do not, I beg of you, desecrate and vulgarize this sacred edifice with speech and behaviour befitting a saloon bar or the local *kinema.*

JACKSON (*appealing to the others and moving to the* PRODUCER'S *chair*). Listen to him. Just listen to him. Did you ever hear such drivel? And what's more, he *knows* it's drivel. The awful part is— he almost convinces me that it isn't.

(*He flops into the* PRODUCER'S *chair.*)

PRODUCER (*roaring*). Get out of my chair.

(JACKSON *rises quickly.*)

Now come along. Come along. Jacko's said his little piece, and he's said it very nicely. We've all had lots of fun and *lots* of games, but "*the play's the thing.*" Work—work—work. (*An afterthought.*) I'll be with you in a minute.

(*He departs from the box.*)

JACKSON (*almost staggering to his chair*). I can't do it. I can't go on. Mary. What did I do with the Aspirin? (*He sits and buries his head in his hands.*)

(MARY *rises and grabs the bottle from the prompt table.*)

MARY. Here they are, Mr Harley.
JACKSON. How many are there left?
MARY. Six.
JACKSON. Well, go to the chemist and buy one; I need seven. If only they were arsenic.

(MARY *exits quickly* L. MAUD *rises and moves to the prompt table.*)

MAUD. "We must all be very kind to one another."

JACKSON (*looking up; surprised*). What's biting *you?*

MAUD. It's just a line from some play or other.

(JACKSON *groans.*)

Oh, come on, Jacko, don't let Harry get you down like that.

JACKSON. And I thought we were getting rid of him for six or seven weeks at least. The doctor definitely promised me . . . (*Wildly.*) I'll kill that doctor when I see him.

(MAUD *breaks up* L. *The* AUTHOR *enters up* R. *and moves* C. *He is vaguely studying some papers he is holding.*)

(*He rises and moves to the* AUTHOR.) Listen, old boy, where did you come from?

AUTHOR. The gentleman's. . . .

JACKSON. No, no, no. I mean, where do you live?

AUTHOR (*puzzled*). Er—Exeter.

JACKSON (*in anguish*). Exeter. Lovely old city. The cathedral. The river. The market square. The *peace*. The quiet. (*He takes both the* AUTHOR's *hands.*) You must go back there, old boy, you must, *you must*, YOU MUST.

AUTHOR (*solemnly*). Oh, but I shall, I shall, I shall.

JACKSON (*pathetically*). But why not go back now—while you're still sane?

AUTHOR (*babbling*). But—but . . .

JACKSON. You don't want to go back to your wife and children a raving lunatic, do you?

AUTHOR. But, Mr Harley, I'm not married. I haven't got a wife and children.

JACKSON (*wearily*). You haven't got a . . . (*His mouth closes, he is too tired to bother any more.*) No, of course, you wouldn't have. All right. (*He pats the mystified* AUTHOR *on the back.*) We won't talk about it any more. (*He moves to the prompt table and flops in his chair, burying his head in his hands once more.*)

(*The* PRODUCER *enters breezily through the stalls door, the* AUTHOR *eases down* R.)

PRODUCER. Now, come along. Come along. We're getting along very nicely, but there's still lots to do. "Once more unto the breach, dear friends, once more. Or close the wall up with our English dead." (*He mounts the steps and crosses the bridge.*)

MAUD (*screaming*). Aaaaah!

PRODUCER (*very casually*). I must get a handrail put on this bridge. (*He moves* C.)

MAUD (*feebly*). A handrail.

PRODUCER (*briskly*). Now. Attention, everybody. I've been thinking quite a lot about this play during the last three-quarters of an hour. . . .

JACKSON (*flabbergasted*). You've been *what*?

PRODUCER. You heard what I said, Jacko, I don't mumble. And I have come to the very definite conclusion that the only way to get this play over, is as a Costume Play.

(*There is a general horrified gasp.*)

AUTHOR (*squeaking*). A *what*?

PRODUCER. Perhaps my diction *isn't* quite as good as I thought. (*Patiently to the* AUTHOR.) A Costume Play, my dear sir, you know —wigs and things. (*He makes vague gestures.*)

(*There is a general babel of protest from the whole Company, out of which* JERRY's *voice is heard.*)

JERRY. It'll kill my "What a wotter" line.

PRODUCER. Thank God for that.

AUTHOR (*moving to* R. *of the* PRODUCER). But, Mr Blacker—how can you alter the period in this way? There's that scene where Melisande is brought in after being run over by a motor car.

PRODUCER. I see no reason why she shouldn't be run over by a sedan chair.

JACKSON (*rising and moving to* L. *of the* PRODUCER). Harry, for Heaven's sake pull yourself together. I don't give a damn whether Melisande is run over by a motor car, a sedan chair, or a Roman chariot. What I'm thinking is this. Today's Wednesday. This play's got to go on on Monday. If you start monkeying about with the damn thing now, it's going to mean a change of scene, ordering of costumes, alteration of dialogue, and God knows what. I tell you, Harry, it's a physical impossibility.

(*There is a pause.*)

PRODUCER (*strolling down* R.). I remember once when I was with Matheson Lang.

(*The* AUTHOR *stamps angrily up* C. JACKSON *moves wearily to his chair and sits.*)

(*He turns and strolls* L.) We were rehearsing *Hamlet* at the time. My wife was playing Ophelia, the lady I was living with at the time —her name escapes me at the moment—was playing the Queen. (*He turns and strolls* R.) Lang came down to rehearsal two days before we opened——

(GEORGE *enters* L.)

—and said to his stage director——

GEORGE (*seeing the* PRODUCER, *and speaking in amazement*). Gawd, strike me pink.

PRODUCER. —Gawd, strike me pink. (*He turns quickly.*) Who said that? (*He sees* GEORGE.) What do you want?

GEORGE (*babbling*). But—but—I thought you was dead.

PRODUCER. God give me patience. What do you want?

GEORGE. I knew it was too good to be true. (*Then bluntly.*) That backcloth.

PRODUCER. What backcloth? What are you talking about?

GEORGE. That grotto backcloth. You want one painting for next week, don't you?

PRODUCER. Well, what about it?

GEORGE (*shouting*). Well, I gotter get it.

PRODUCER (*striding* C.). Well, get it, man, get it. But for Heaven's sake don't worry me about the damn thing.

GEORGE. All right, all right, so long as we know. (*As he moves* L.) Gawd stone the crows.

(GEORGE *exits* L.)

PRODUCER. Of all the incompetent stupid fools. Now, where was I?

JACKSON (*imploringly*). Don't tell him, anyone.

PRODUCER. Ah, yes, I remember.

AUTHOR (*moving down to* R. *of the* PRODUCER). Mr Blacker, I must speak.

JACKSON (*rising and moving* L. *of the* PRODUCER). Yes, and so must I. Harry, if you go through with this mad-brained idea of yours, I quit. Get that? I quit.

NORWOOD. And that goes for me, too—and my wife. Do you realize that she's got a part as long as *Back to Methuselah* to learn?

(*Everyone joins in, protesting. The hubbub gets louder and louder.*)

PRODUCER (*interrupting; walking out on to the bridge and standing with his back to the audience*). You blocks. You stones. You worse than senseless things. Don't you realize that what I propose doing is for your own good? Do you want to go on to this stage on Monday next and be howled off? (*He strides back between the* AUTHOR *and* JACKSON.) I have a reputation as a producer.

JACKSON. You have—and it stinks.

PRODUCER (*rounding on* JACKSON). You'll get a letter from my solicitors first thing in the morning. You know as well as I do that this is the most God awful play it's ever been our misfortune to put on in this theatre.

AUTHOR (*angrily*). Mr Blacker . . .

PRODUCER. Shut up.

(*A large backcloth begins to descend slowly from the flies, above the* PRODUCER, *the* AUTHOR *and* JACKSON.)

AUTHOR. Mr Blacker, you will receive a letter from *my* solicitors in the morning.

JACKSON. Look, Harry, we know this play's no damn good, but . . .

AUTHOR (*incensed*). You, too, will receive a letter from my solicitors.

JACKSON. Oh, shut up.

(*The backcloth continues to descend. It is now seen to be a pantomime cloth.*)

(*To the* PRODUCER.) Then why not scrap it altogether?

PRODUCER. No.

JACKSON (*striding* L.). Very well, then, *I quit*.

PRODUCER. All right then, *quit*.

(JACKSON *looks a bit shaken but exits* L. *The* PRODUCER *moves down stage.*)

This play is billed, and it goes on—as I say it goes on.

AUTHOR. Over my dead——

(*The cloth comes down to the stage and the* AUTHOR *disappears from sight. The* PRODUCER *is left alone in front of the cloth.*)

(*He shouts.*) —body.

(*From behind the cloth come shouts and protests. The* PRODUCER *is quite unconscious of what has happened. He paces up and down the footlights, never looking up stage.*)

PRODUCER (*loudly*). You can shout. You can yell. But as long as I am the producer in this theatre, my word is law. I've stood for a good deal this morning. I've had things said to me and done to me that would have broken the spirit of a lesser man. But not me. Always, always, *I am Caesar*. (*He turns and sees the cloth.*) What the hell's this? Who did this? *Who did this?* This is the end.

AUTHOR (*banging the* R. *end of the cloth*). Mr Blacker, can you hear me?

PRODUCER (*shouting through the cloth*). No. (*He shouts in the direction of the flies.*) George.

GEORGE (*from the flies; unruffled*). 'Ullo?

AUTHOR (*still banging the cloth from behind*). Can you hear me *now*, Mr Blacker?

PRODUCER (*furiously; slapping the cloth hard where the* AUTHOR *is hitting it.*) Don't do *that*.

(*There is a yell of pain from the* AUTHOR.)

(*He shouts into the flies again.*) George, did you lower this cloth?

GEORGE (*from the flies*). 'Course I did.

AUTHOR (*from behind the* L. *end of the cloth, and banging it*). Mr Blacker, you struck me in the presence of witnesses.

PRODUCER (*shouting at the* R. *end of the cloth and banging it*). Will you be quiet when I'm taking a rehearsal?

AUTHOR (*still at the* L. *end*). No, sir, I will not be quiet. I warn you, if you tamper any further with my play . . .

PRODUCER. What play? You haven't written a play yet.
AUTHOR. I am a patient man, but . . .

(*The lowering of the cloth is resumed and the top batten appears. The cloth is hung on lines at either end. The centre line also descends, but it is free of the cloth and has a large sandbag on the end of it.*)

PRODUCER (*shouting to the flies*). George, if you don't get this cloth out of the way in two minutes, I'll come up there and pitch you down on to the stage.

(*The top batten of the cloth is now about half-way down to the stage.*)

GEORGE (*derisively from the flies*). Oh, you will, will you? Well, you'll get a letter from my solicitors in the morning.

(*The top batten of the cloth comes right down to the stage. The sandbag stops at about head height. The AUTHOR disentangles himself from the folds of the cloth at the R. end of it.*)

AUTHOR. Now, sir, will you listen to me?
PRODUCER (*running up the steps R.C. and pulling the AUTHOR bodily up on to the rostrum*). No, sir, *you* will listen to *me*.

(*The company watch, horrified. NORWOOD, JERRY and AVIS are up C. SANDRA is R. of the table, DAPHNE above the table, and MAUD L. of the table.*)

(*His face almost touches the AUTHOR's, he spits the words through clenched teeth.*)

"I do not love thee, Doctor Fell
The reason why I cannot tell
But this I know—and know full well
I do not love thee, Doctor Fell."

(*The PRODUCER gives a burst of mad laughter. The AUTHOR's hat falls off.*)

MAUD (*distractedly*). He's gone mad. I knew it would happen. He's gone mad.
PRODUCER (*to the AUTHOR; fuming*). You know as well as I do that if your grandmother hadn't been a director of this theatre, your play would never have seen the light of day.
AUTHOR (*squeakily*). I resent that.
PRODUCER. *You* resent it. *I* resent it. I resent that my judgement should be overruled by a silly old woman who falls asleep ten minutes after she gets into the theatre and when she goes out doesn't know whether she's seen *The Merry Wives of Windsor* or *Annie Get Your Gun*. (*He hurls the AUTHOR down the steps.*)
AUTHOR (*livid*). You shall suffer for this, Mr Blacker. I will see my aunt in the morning. I'll have you thrown out of this theatre. (*He backs away waving his arms.*) I'll have you hounded out of this

town, I'll have you . . . (*His arm knocks against the sandbag hanging on the centre line. He swings it and sends it at the* PRODUCER.)

(*The* PRODUCER *catches the bag.*)

PRODUCER (*throwing the bag back at the* AUTHOR). Don't do *that*.

(*The sandbag crashes into the* AUTHOR. *He reels back, catches his foot in the top batten of the cloth, trips and falls back on his head. He lies still on the stage. There is a horrified exclamation from the Company, and then silence.*)

MAUD (*after a pause*). Now look what you've done.

PRODUCER (*after a pause; descending the steps and moving down* R.). I remember when I was with Tod Slaughter . . .

(*The Company crowd round the fallen* AUTHOR. *The* PRODUCER *continues to talk to himself.* NORWOOD *retrieves the* AUTHOR's *hat. Then two* AMBULANCE MEN *enter up* R. DAPHNE's *dog rushes all over the place excitedly.* MARY *enters down* L. *There is pandemonium. The* AMBULANCE MEN, *carrying a stretcher, see the fallen* AUTHOR *and bring the stretcher down to him.*)

1ST AMBULANCE MAN. It's all right. It's all right. We'll take care of him now.

(*The* AMBULANCE MEN *lift the* AUTHOR *on to the stretcher. The cast are stupefied for a moment. Then pandemonium breaks out again.* DAPHNE *begins to have hysterics and is assisted to the chair* R. *of the table by* MAUD *and* AVIS. JERRY *fans* DAPHNE.)

DAPHNE. They're not going to . . . (*Hysterically.*) I can't stand it. I can't stand it. (*She goes off into shrieks of laughter.*)

1ST AMBULANCE MAN. Right, Jim.

(*The* AMBULANCE MEN *lift the stretcher.*)

PRODUCER (*taking* AUTHOR's *hat away from* NORWOOD; *calmly*). One moment. (*He places the hat reverently on the recumbent body of the* AUTHOR.)

(*The* AMBULANCE MEN *take the* AUTHOR *off up* R. *As they exit,* JACKSON *enters down* L. *He has on his overcoat, carries a large suitcase, and a bag of golf clubs. He moves to the bridge, crosses it, and starts towards the stalls door. The* PRODUCER *moves on to the bridge and shouts to* JACKSON.)

PRODUCER. Where the hell are *you* going?

JACKSON. I'm going back to the R.A.F.

(*He exits through the stalls door.*)

PRODUCER. Good. Now perhaps we *can* get on. (*He turns and faces the stage.*) All right, stand by, everyone. Act One, beginners, please.

(*The* CURTAIN *comes down quickly, leaving the* PRODUCER *on the bridge in front of it. He turns to the audience.*)

PRODUCER. Well, that's it. I'm sorry if you've had a boring time, but I did warn you, didn't I? Of course, you've been rather unlucky. You happen to have struck a particularly dull rehearsal. Sometimes tempers get very frayed and we have the most appalling scenes. But that doesn't happen very often, thank goodness. On the whole we jog along in the happy-go-lucky way you've seen this morning, and I think I can say we're one of the happiest little repertory companies in the country. Oh, one thing more. May I remind you, as you go out, don't forget to book your seats for next Monday's really big attraction. The first performance on any stage of an entirely new play entitled *The Morals of Melisande* by Augustus Sidebottom.

He bows and steps back. The CURTAIN *rises and the company are lined up for the calls. The* PRODUCER *takes his place in the middle of the line.*

FURNITURE AND PROPERTY PLOT

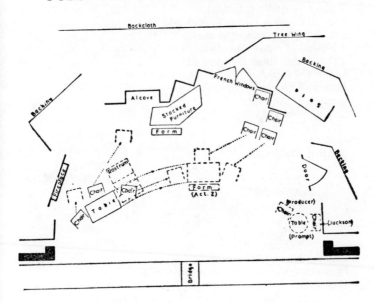

Throughout the play:

ACT I

On stage:
Rough table.
5 bentwood chairs.
2 ornate chairs.
6 ft. wooden form.
Door.
Sofa.
Stacked furniture.
Dust sheets.
Recessed french window flat.
Alcove flat.
Fireplace flat.
2 4-ft. flats.
2 Backings.
Tree wing.
2 Backcloths.

Stage lamps, ladders, etc. (*Dressing.*)
Standard lamp. Pedestal with bust. Curtains. (*Dressing for french window recess.*)
Vase of flowers. (*Dressing for alcove.*)

Off stage:
Gong and stick (JACKSON).
Rostrum with 3 treads (JACKSON).
Small prompt table (MARY).
2 bentwood chairs (MARY).
4 ft. wooden form (for ACT II).
Letter (MAUD).
Basket of groceries (MAUD).
3 letters (DAPHNE).
Setting plan (MARY).

Personal:
Scripts: PRODUCER.
         MAUD.
         JERRY.
         AUTHOR.
         DAPHNE.
         AVIS.
         JACKSON.
         SANDRA.
         NORWOOD.
PRODUCER: Sundry papers, wrist-watch.
JERRY: Scarf, letter, cigarettes, lighter.
MAUD: Handbag. *In it:* cuttings, handkerchief.
AUTHOR: Pince-nez, umbrella, brief-case.
AVIS: Handbag. *In it:* handkerchief.
DAPHNE: Sling bag. *In it:* purse with coins, cigarettes, lighter, compact, lipstick, handkerchief.
JACKSON: Board with papers and clip, blue pencil, cigarettes, lighter.
GEORGE: Chalk, rule, setting plan, hammer, cigarettes, matches, handkerchief.

ACT II

Set 4 ft. wooden form below table.

Off stage:
Letter (NORWOOD).
Glass of water (JACKSON).
Bottle of Aspirins (JACKSON).
Lampshade (MARY).
Letter (JACKSON).

Newspaper (NORWOOD).
Tray with 6 cups of coffee (MARY).
Jug of coffee (MAUD).

Personal:
    SANDRA: Handbag. *In it:* compact, lighter, cigarettes.
    NORWOOD: Cigarettes, lighter.
    PRODUCER: Coins, handkerchief.
    JERRY: Eyeglass.

ACT III

Off stage:
    Bandages (AUTHOR).
    Bottle of iodine (AUTHOR).
    Cottonwool (AUTHOR).
    Stretcher.
    Overcoat (JACKSON).
    Suitcase (JACKSON).
    Golf clubs (JACKSON).

Personal:
    PRODUCER: Head bandage, arm sling.
    AUTHOR: Loose roll of bandage.
    DOCTOR. Medical bag.

The correct costumes and wigs used in the production of this play may be obtained from Messrs Charles H. Fox Ltd, 25 Shelton Street, London WC2H 9HX

LIGHTING PLOT

Battens and floats. 2 circuits. 52.
                            1 circuit. 7.
                            1 circuit. Open white.
                            Spots. 51 and 52.
                            F.O.H. 51 and 52.

ACT I

To open. Working light on.

At cue. PRODUCER: . . . the cast do that—House lights and stage lights—full up.

At cue. PRODUCER: . . . on this thing one day—House lights out.

ACT II

To open. Stage lights—full up.

At cue. PRODUCER (*calling*): Jacko—Black out.

At cue. PRODUCER: . . . break my neck. Help. Stage lights—full up.

At cue. PRODUCER: Tell him I'm coming—Black out.

ACT III

To open. Stage lights—full up

No cue.

*2284-1
1981
5-07
C